Dearest Sis Ellie,

Enjoy reading the Word of GOD.

Bit by bit is a spiritual fit

Love,
Sis Esther

Happy Birthday!

Bible Tidbits

By

Esther B. Jimenez

1663 LIBERTY DRIVE, SUITE 200
BLOOMINGTON, INDIANA 47403
(800) 839-8640
WWW.AUTHORHOUSE.COM

© 2004 Esther B. Jimenez.
All Rights Reserved.

No part of this book may be reproduced, stored in a retrieval system, or transmitted by any means without the written permission of the author.

First published by AuthorHouse 12/07/04

ISBN: 1-4184-6864-9 (e)
ISBN: 1-4184-5056-1 (sc)

Printed in the United States of America
Bloomington, Indiana

This book is printed on acid-free paper.

Book and Cover Design by Esther B. Jimenez

DEDICATION

To my two grandchildren
Christian Jay M. Jimenez
Elaiza Jelyn M. Jimenez

To my nephews and nieces
Jay, Ralph Jr., Jan Carlo,
Paul Christian, Francis John "Chikoy"
Rona Liza, Joyce Elizabeth, and
Esther Charisse "Chini".

PREFACE

My book is not a love story, but a story of how to love in a Christian way.

My book is written not by a theologian, but by an ordinary person who was given the grace of courage to share GOD's wonder of wonders.

My book is not fiction, but a reflection of the Scriptures through my life's experiences. I just unwrapped one of the Holy Spirit's gifts, that I received, that is, the birth of the Bible Tidbits.

I chose the title, "BIBLE TIDBITS", because every bit that the Bible conveys is pleasing to the soul, with all its moral lessons, stories and experiences of the people in the Old Testament and in the New Testament; the prophecies and their fulfillment; the miracles, the parables, the healing, the teaching and the preaching of our LORD and much more. "Bit By Bit Is A Spiritual Fit". Bible Tidbits is based on Scriptural passages that inspired me. Each page has a Scriptural passage, with my reflection on each passage. Then, my fervent prayer after each reflection.

There are 101 Bible Tidbits that will keep you enlightened. You can read a page a day, the whole book in a day, or any way you want to read it. But the key here is to find out too, what Scriptural passages inspire you. Maybe there'll be a message for you that will prompt you to share.

Let me share with you a stanza from one of my poems entitled, "Amazing Book".

If you're weary, tired, worried and troubled,
Just open your Bible and ponder on the Scriptures;
There are wonderful passages that the Bible offers,
And your tribulations will turn into triumphs

(The rests of the Amazing Book poem is found in the 101st Bible Tidbits)

TABLE OF CONTENTS

DEDICATION v

PREFACE vii

ACKNOWLEDGEMENTS xv

FOREWORD xvii

REVIEW FROM THE EDITORS xxi

INTRODUCTORY PRAYER xxiii

JESUS IS IN YOU AND ME 1

THE VOICE OF GOD IS A ROARING THUNDER 2

HONORING 3

ACCEPTANCE…AS A GIFT 4

WHEN GOD MEANT BUSINESS HE REALLY MEANT BUSINESS 5

TRAFFIC CONTROLLER 6

A DRIVER'S PRAYER 7

WEEDS PULLER 8

MASTER BUILDER 9

THE ROOT OF ALL EVIL 10

WHAT MORE CAN WE ASK? 11

THE ARMOR OF GOD 12

PRIDE VS. HUMILITY 13

VANITY OF VANITIES 14

PROMISES CAN BE BROKEN 15

"IT IS I"	16
WHAT A PRIVILEGE?	17
ONE WAY STREET TO PEACE	18
CHILDREN ARE US	19
POWERFUL SEED	20
BEHIND THE TRUTH	21
GOD IS WITH US	22
SHEEP'S GATE	23
GENEROSITY	24
LOSING IS GAINING	25
THE BEST ADVERTISING	26
THE ESSENCE OF FAITH	27
FREE CHOICE	28
MEDITATION VS. REFLECTION	29
HANDMAIDS OF THE LORD	30
MARCH WITH GOD	31
SOLDIERS' PRAYER	32
FORGIVE, HOW MANY TIMES?	33
LOVE COUNTS	34
THE FAITHFUL ONE	35
ACTION SPEAKS THE TRUTH	36
PROPER ENDORSEMENT	37
THE MAP OF LIFE	38

WILLINGNESS	39
CHALLENGES IN LIFE	40
OUR COMPASS TO ETERNAL LIFE	41
THE LORD'S DAY	42
REAR VIEW MIRROR	43
THE LIGHT OF OUR LIVES	44
DISCIPLINE	45
BETWEEN ALPHABET LETTERS	46
HUNGER AND THIRST	47
PASS OR FAIL	48
INCENTIVE	49
CELIBACY	50
POOR VS. RICH	51
THE WAY TO SAINTHOOD	52
THE SOURCE	53
SANCTUARY	54
ROAD TO SALVATION	55
TAME YOUR TONGUE	56
IN JESUS NAME	57
PRAISE THE ALMIGHTY	58
BE PREPARED	59
SIMPLE REQUEST	60
LAST WORDS	61

FOOTPRINTS	62
THE RESCUER	63
INSEPARABLE	64
MIND OUR OWN BUSINESS	65
THE BEST CHOICE	66
CONSTRUCTIVE CRITICISM	67
ANIMALS AND PETS	68
BE ASSERTIVE…IN A CHRISTIAN WAY	69
HOLY REPLACEMENT	70
LENGTHEN THE LENT SEASON	71
GENUINE FRIENDSHIP	72
PERSONAL APPEARANCE	73
DEGREE OF LOVE	74
RENEWED LIFE	75
BEYOND CONTROL	76
PATHWAY OF THE JUST	77
THE REAL QUENCHER	78
THE BEST INVITATION	79
HUMILITY	80
DESIRE TO SERVE	81
COURAGEOUS WOMAN	83
GOD'S DIVINE STRATEGY	84
FEED THE NEEDY	85

REMEMBER!!! TO FORGET	86
RESPECT	87
EXPERIENCE IS THE BEST TEACHER	88
YOUR CHANCE AND MINE	89
COME O HOLY SPIRIT, COME	90
GOD'S CALENDAR	91
A WIN – WIN SITUATION	92
LIVING WATER	93
THE WORD	94
COME TO THE RESCUE	95
CO - DEPENDENCY	96
PASS WITH FLYING COLORS	97
NO EXCEPTION	98
SALT OF THE EARTH	99
PACKAGE DEAL	100
THE STUMP	101
MODEL OF HUMILITY	102
THE POWER OF INTERCESSION	103
UNDERSTANDING THE SCRIPTURES	104
EXTRA TIDBIT	105
GOD'S PROMISE	106
APPRECIATION	107

ACKNOWLEDGEMENTS

I want to thank a lot of people who have contributed towards having the Bible Tidbits published.

First, my sincerest thanks to my family,(parents, brothers, my sister, in-laws, nieces and nephews), who have been very supportive and have believed in me. Thanks to my cousin Beth, who has shared her spiritual ears, listening while I was reading my manuscript for verbal editing.

My sincere appreciation to Brother Charles Madden who gave his time to edit my book from cover to cover. I learned from him the importance of accuracy and presenting a book professionally.

To Father John Grigus who shared selflessly his precious moments to ponder on some of the chapters in my book. He gladly gave his feedback and encouraged me to go on and share the gift that GOD Has given me.

I wish to extend my gratitude to the editors who reviewed my manuscript and helped me decide to have it published.

There are more relatives and friends that I would like to acknowledge. They are the key to the completion of the Bible Tidbits. A book must have a beginning and an end. Their names are the completion of this book and they are listed at the end. THANKS TO ALL!

FOREWORD

In his Apostolic Letter, "At the Beginning of the Third Millennium," Pope John II identifies the study and reflective listening to the word of Scriptures to be a chief pastoral priority to be engaged in by all the baptized for the purpose of growing in deeper holiness of life. "It is especially necessary that listening to the word of GOD should become a life-giving encounter, in the ancient and ever valid tradition of *lectio divina"*, says the Holy Father, "which draws from the Biblical text the living word which questions, directs and shapes our lives" (*Novo Millennio Inuente,* 38).

Through the influence of divine grace Esther Jimenez seems to have been taught how to do this in a very personal yet natural and spontaneous way. In these "Bible Tidbits" she now not only shares the wealth of this personal reflection with others but teaches how any person regardless of his or her walk of life or educational background can make the daily reading of Scriptures a life-giving experience. Though short and simple, these "Bible Tidbits" are truly impactful!

I recommend this book to anyone. It will especially appeal to those whose lives are very busy and who feel that they do not have much time to spend in a more in-depth study of GOD's word but who long to take a kernel of the truth present there and conform their lives to it on a daily basis.

Fr. John P. Grigus, OFM Conv
Director of Marytown's Perpetual Adoration Program
and Media Communications Ministry
Libertyville, Illinois

ABOUT THE AUTHOR

Estrella "aka " Esther B. Jimenez, is a native of Manila, Philippines, a nurse by profession, a US immigrant and has been in the USA for almost 25 years.

Esther is a parishioner of St. Peter, the Apostle of Itasca, Illinois; a Eucharistic Minister of the same church. She had been a member of the parish council for three years..

She had offered spiritual reflections on the topics of Holiness, Prayer, Christianity and the Holy Spirit in her community.

She had one book self-published four years ago (2000) entitled, "365 Days Food For Thoughts".

She is working on the following:
    (1) What's In My heart? (Spiritual and Inspirational Poems)
    (2) Daily Graces (Prayers before meals)
    (3) Words To Live By, For Nurses

In her leisure time, she paints scenery, (landscape - nature) plays guitar, writes, reads and for holistic therapy she goes fishing. She does some volunteer jobs.

She is currently making inspirational cards printed on her paintings. Esther believes in... "the mind speaks from the heart".

REVIEW FROM THE EDITORS

Inspirational in nature, Esther B. Jimenez' Bible Tidbits is an uplifting, challenging and thought-provoking read. This is a collection that forces the reader to a re-evaluation of life and the values we apply to it in our daily thoughts and actions. If we were all to slow down a little, and think more deeply how GOD would react to our behavior and our thought processes, we might be able to regulate our lives more closely according to the ways that He showed us through His Son, JESUS CHRIST.

Frequently taking a commonplace saying or opinion that will be familiar to the reading audience, Esther B. Jimenez develops that thought or theme to a deeper level, encouraging the readers to see their own lives reflected in her words, and their own souls reflected in the mirror that GOD holds up to their actions. Only in this way can we grow as His children, and begin to become more worthy of His love and presence in our lives.

Referring always to Scripture, she follows that up with practical advice that her readers can easily understand and relate to within the context of their own daily existence, so that GOD's Word becomes part of the very fabric of life in all its many wondrous forms. I would like to see Esther B. Jimenez' work available to the general reading public.

A. Austen

After reading the material, the following are my comments:
1. the reflections are brief and concise, very reader-friendly and written in a manner for easy understanding.
2. the author has made use of examples to which many people irrespective of culture, can easily relate.
3. her insights are inspiring and heart-warming, reflecting the author's own inclination toward meditation on GOD's love and other matters of the spirit.
4. the author's efforts to provoke her readers to challenge themselves and look deeper into their hearts is commendable.

Maria Victoria Lucero

INTRODUCTORY PRAYER

LORD GOD, Heavenly Father, I thank You for allowing me to use the gifts that You have given me, the gift of knowledge and the gift of wisdom.

You are an awesome, generous and a forgiving GOD, and I honor You with profound reverence.

May You touch the readers while they "Bit By Bit" read the Biblical messages and the inspiring words from You.

I am offering the Bible Tidbits to You LORD, to Your Son, to the Holy Spirit and to our Blessed Virgin Mary.

Again, thank You for Your endless blessings and graces.

LORD, You are always blessing me with Your love and mercy, and I am very grateful for that.

I love You my LORD and I bless You for everything, in JESUS' name, I pray, Amen!

JESUS IS IN YOU AND ME

John 20: 15

JESUS said to her, "Woman, why are you weeping? Whom are you looking for?" She thought it was the gardener and said to him, "Sir, if you carried him away, tell me where you laid him, and I will take him".

We should see JESUS in everyone's face. When JESUS was resurrected on the third day, no one recognized Him and Mary Magdala, one of the first people who saw Him, thought He was a gardener. So if she thought JESUS was a gardener, just remember that JESUS is in everyone's face. The truth is, we have to be aware of our surroundings, the people we encounter and the way we treat people. The Presence of JESUS is in our hearts all the time.

Mother Teresa saw JESUS many, many times in her life, through the faces of the poorest of the poor. JESUS is indeed in you and me.

LORD GOD, may You give me a heart to recognize and acknowledge You in everyone's face. If I am faced with my enemy, let me see You in him, so I can handle it divinely and I can only do this LORD with Your grace, in JESUS' name, I pray, Amen!
07/27/01

Esther B. Jimenez

THE VOICE OF GOD IS A ROARING THUNDER

Exodus 19: 19

The trumpet blast grew louder and louder, while Moses was speaking and GOD answering him with thunder.

Thunder and lightning, these are two of GOD's creations, and some of us are scared that we might be stricken if we don't avoid them. We really can't avoid them because they are part of nature.

News on every television and radio station tells us about people struck by lightning.

What I am trying to say is, the antidote for thunder-lightning phobia is to just think that GOD is giving messages to us.

So let us be silent and let's pray the next time thunder roars and lightning strikes.

Remember, when GOD gave the Ten Commandments to Moses it was with thunder and electrifying lightning.

LORD GOD, I am one of Your creations, who is indeed scared of thunder and lightning. I know LORD that they are part of nature, and whatever You created serves a purpose. The next time I hear the thunder, may You give me the gift of wisdom to know what Your message is. May I see the true light in lightning, in JESUS' name I pray.
07/27/01

HONORING

John 12: 3

Mary took a liter of costly perfumed oil made from genuine aromatic nard and anointed the feet of JESUS and dried them with her hair; the house was filled with the fragrance of the oil.

When someone dies, it is a customary in most cases to give a "eulogy", honoring the person during the funeral service. Too bad the person can't hear those honoring words given by his/her friends and loved ones anymore.

Mary indeed prepared something expensive because she knew that the Person she would honor would pay a great price. This preparation was before JESUS' death, in which later would give up His life for us. So, this is how we should honor someone we love, or someone close to us, not when they're gone, but while they're still with us.

LORD GOD, Heavenly Father, may I have the honor to tell You how I am grateful for creating me in Your Image and nurturing me as I grew up physically and spiritually. LORD, thank You for this important message from the Holy Book, that I may start saying, "I love you" to the people I love and care. I pray in JESUS' name, Amen!

07/28/01

Esther B. Jimenez

ACCEPTANCE…AS A GIFT

Isaiah 30 : 15
For thus said the LORD GOD, the Holy One of Israel: By waiting and by calm you shall be saved, in quiet and in trust strength lies: But this you did not wish.

    A few months ago, I received a call from one of my best friends, a classmate of mine in Nursing. She is in California now. We have been keeping in touch for the past seven years. As soon as she mentioned the words, "bad news Es", I suspected it's a physical/health issue. I was right, she was diagnosed as having cancer of the breast. It shook me, but I tried to sound strong over the phone. We cried and there was some silence in between our conversation. After a few days, she updated me on how things were going. She decided not to have surgery or other oncologic procedures. She even emphasized that instead of focusing her thoughts on "radiation" and "chemotherapy", she'll just continue to serve her clients that are in her two retirement homes. She strongly believed that there is a reason for everything including her cancer. Then a few days after, we talked again.
    And this time, I could hardly grasp her amazing plans. She had already made necessary plans for her funeral, including her assets, burial, tombstone and even the casket. For a while I thought my friend was in denial. But no, she is resigned to whatever the will of GOD is for her. Her trust and faith makes her stronger. I admire her spiritual boldness. Her acceptance of her illness is a "Blessing", a "Gift" that she can treasure because she is given a chance to prepare for her peaceful destination.

> LORD GOD, Heavenly Father, I am thanking You for giving her to me as my friend. May You continue to guide her every step of the way LORD. You work in mysterious ways and I believe that miracles happen. Grant her LORD peace in her heart. Whatever she feels and wherever she is, may You give her the grace of calmness and grant the gift of spiritual tenacity, in JESUS' name I pray, Amen!

09/10/02 (Late Entry)

WHEN GOD MEANT BUSINESS HE REALLY MEANT BUSINESS

Genesis 18 : 24

Suppose there were fifty innocent people in the city; would you wipe out the place, rather than spare it for the sake of fifty innocent within it?

In business if you don't know your stuff and if you don't know how to negotiate, you'll lose the business. When Abraham started negotiating about sparing the whole city, he started the figure from fifty down, then to at least ten innocent people. GOD agreed to every condition, provided there was really an innocent person, but there was none.

In our lives, we tend to continuously bargain with GOD. GOD knows our hearts and so we don't need to be repetitive in our plea. Just be honest and be humble.

And GOD wants us to use these two virtues, (humility and honesty) in any business transactions that you have daily.

LORD GOD, there are times I procrastinate over things that I need to do, and I ask You LORD, for Your understanding. May You give me the grace of self-discipline, to handle Your "business" in a divine way. Thank You for the "holy business", in JESUS' name I pray, Amen!
07/29/01

Esther B. Jimenez

TRAFFIC CONTROLLER

Jeremiah 42 : 3

"Let the LORD, your GOD, show us what way we should take and what we should do".

Our trials in life is like traffic, and sometimes we think of how we can get out, or which way to a short cut, or which alternative way to use, to avoid it. Not only that, traffic aggravates a lot of people.

In my life, I feel like I am always stuck in traffic. I get tense and irritated. But I fail to realize that all I need to do is to leave everything in GOD's hands and His directions. He will give us the right pathway. So any struggles, confusions, trials and any sort of problems you have, always offer them to the LORD Almighty. He is our "Traffic Controller".

LORD GOD, Heavenly Father, in my moments of discernment, please be with me and be there as my traffic light and my traffic controller. Thank You for Your guidance and direction. LORD, please give me the gift of patience that I need, to stay calm when I am caught in traffic, I ask this in JESUS' name, Amen!
07/30/01

A DRIVER'S PRAYER

LORD, thank You for another day today,
To witness Your wonder of wonders;
Thank You for being my co-driver,
You are indeed a Great Protector.
May You grant me a safe hand
To be gentle in my driving;
May You give me the grace of patience,
In dealing with the traffic scene,
When I'm sleepy and feel uneasy,
Please wake me up and extend Your hands,
Embrace me with Your love and warmth
Until I reach my destination
And be with me LORD till I get home,
LORD, thank You too, for an angel of my own,
In JESUS' name, I pray Amen!

Esther B. Jimenez

WEEDS PULLER

Matthew 13 : 40

Just as weeds are collected and burned up with fire, so will it be at the end of the age.

Have you focused your mind on the weeds that come out, especially if you are into gardening?

Have you seen the TV commercial about how this person pulls the weeds out from his lawn? He even use machinery. How about the one spraying the weeds with certain chemicals?

Weeds are obstacles in our spiritual growth. The vices, the vanities, the obsessions, the addictions and many more, are the weeds in our lives. We can only take those weeds out through GOD's grace. Remember, He is the greatest "Weeds Puller". You don't need to use big machinery nor a chemical spray. Will you let the Weeds Puller handle the weeds in your life?

> LORD GOD, I know and You know that I have a lot of weeds to pull out in my life. I thank You for helping me pull those weeds out. Please continue O LORD, to be my Weeds Puller, in JESUS' name, I pray, Amen!
> 07/31/01

Bible Tidbits

MASTER BUILDER

1 Corinthians 3 : 10-11

10 According to the grace of GOD given to me, like a wise master builder I laid a foundation, and another is building upon it. But each must be careful how he builds upon it, 11 for no one can lay a foundation other than the one that is there, namely, JESUS CHRIST.

For us who love to have a house, or own a house, fail to realize that without skilled carpenters, we won't be able to satisfy our desire of having a dream house.

GOD and His Son JESUS really work hand in hand. Our LORD is the Master Builder and our Savior JESUS CHRIST is the Carpenter; and we are the houses, their "dream-houses". Both of them laid strong foundation, in order for us to get into the eternal home, in heaven. So let us be firm in our conviction to do right in GOD's sight.

LORD GOD, You are really our Master Builder and JESUS is our Carpenter. We are the temples that You built. LORD, let me be worthy of Your workmanship, to serve as Your "dream- house", I pray this in JESUS' name, Amen!
07/31/01

Esther B. Jimenez

THE ROOT OF ALL EVIL

Matthew 6 : 24

"No one can serve two masters. He will either hate one and love the other, or be devoted to one and despise the other. You cannot serve GOD and mammon".

"Mammon" is an Aramaic word meaning wealth or property. Nothing is wrong with having money, but what is wrong is focusing on everything you want, the earthly riches. There is an adage that says, "money is the root of all evil." There is truth in this, in some way, but the root of all evil is the "love of money".

In business partnerships, money is sometimes the cause of splitting; in the inheritance of wealth, money is the reason for misunderstanding and family feuds. In the news you often hear, read or watch about robberies, and shooting sprees, money laundering, etc. In short, the wealth, the money become the master of the world. So forget the love of money, the root of all evil. Focus on thinking about the Kingdom of GOD, where the real Master is.

> LORD GOD, I thank You for being our real and genuine Master. You are the One who is always providing our means of livelihood. May You guide us in using our means in a Christian way. I ask the Holy Spirit to grant me the gift of wisdom, and I pray that You may grant me the grace to do Your will. I pray this in JESUS' name Amen!
> 08/01/01

Bible Tidbits

WHAT MORE CAN WE ASK?

Psalm 144 : 1-2

1 Blessed be the LORD, my Rock, who trains my hands for battle, my fingers for war; 2 My safeguard and my fortress, my stronghold, My deliverer, My shield, in whom I trust, who subdues peoples under me.

We are aware that GOD is a good GOD. We know that He provides for everything, like the shelter, the abundance and the protection. We call Him in times of our distress and tribulations, but yet, it seems we are still anxious about everything. Let us dissect these particular verses. "My Rock", how strong is it? Well the strength that we have comes from His strength. He is the Rock of all ages, the GOD Almighty. He is our permanent post that we can lean on forever, the fortress of our lives. He guides us every step of the way and He is our safeguard. Not to forget, He is our Deliverer, the Savior of mankind.

How about, "My Shield?" His shield is our security blanket, our Protector. His shield is warm and it gives us comfort. He is our refuge forever. I could go on and on, but what more can we ask?

> LORD GOD, You are my security and my everything. Thank You for Your greatness, goodness and kindness. Grant me the gift of peace and contentment as You are our Rock and Shield. Your love and mercy is all I ask and I pray this in JESUS' name Amen!
> 08/02/01

Esther B. Jimenez

THE ARMOR OF GOD

Ephesians 6 : 16 – 17

16 In all circumstances, hold faith as a shield, to quench all (the) flaming arrows of the evil one. 17 And take the helmet of salvation and the sword of the Spirit, which is the Word of GOD.

Guns, explosives, grenades, these are defensive weapons that are used in killing. But these don't bother Satan at all. He likes fires and explosives.

One thing he can't capture is our "soul", that is if we have the right weapon, which is "The Armor of GOD". Imagine, if you have the shield of faith, Satan would start avoiding you. If you wear the helmet of salvation no evil whispers would go through. The sword of the Spirit is another strong weapon, because it is the Word of GOD, the Spirit's sword is GOD'S WORD.

These weapons are the holy bullets that you can hold on to. Are you ready to wear the "Armor of GOD?"

These are extra powerful bullets:
- Prayer
- Holy Sacraments
- Saints
- Fasting
- Holy Water
- Rosary
- Eucharist
- Crucifix
- Novena
- Devotions to the Blessed Virgin Mary
- Holy Family and the Holy Trinity

LORD GOD, You are my Armor and my Weapon, thank You for all the holy bullets that I can use to rebuke the temptation and evil whispers and all the abominations that surround us. Thank You for the gifts of the Holy Spirit, and for the constant intercession of Our Blessed Mother, I pray this in JESUS' name Amen!
08/02/01

PRIDE VS. HUMILITY

Psalm 25 : 8 – 9

⁸ Good and upright is the LORD, who shows sinners the way, 9 Guides the humble rightly, and teaches the humble the way.

Come to think of it, we envy the rich people, we despise being poor, but we fail to realize that everything is GOD's plan. He has plans for everyone.

It is the way we handle things that makes the difference. I realize now that the answers to our questions of "why" and "how" really can be found in His Word in the Bible. Imagine the humble will be taught how to handle their lives. And those who acknowledge their nothingness will be guided. So admit that we are nothing without GOD, but we can offer our nothingness to Him. Let us admit too, that we are sinners and we need to amend our faults, and we need to repent for our wrong doings. That's a start! So, what is your choice? To go on with your pride or surrender your pride to GOD?

> LORD GOD, I thank and praise You for creating the poor people, to serve as our model of humility. Grant us LORD the real message of humility. Please make me more humble today than yesterday, and more humble tomorrow than today. All this I pray in JESUS' name Amen!
> 08/05/01

Esther B. Jimenez

VANITY OF VANITIES

Ecclesiastes 1 : 2

Vanity of vanities, say Qoheleth, vanity of vanities! All things are vanity!

Some women can't leave home without make-up on their faces; some men can't have breakfast without a newspaper in front of them; I couldn't go out without hair spraying my hair,(I do now). Some people can't do this, or be without this or without that. We have a lot of vanities in life. These vanities are the results of addiction, attachment and obsession. And these vanities are not even necessary. They are just extra luggage. You may say, "I don't have vanities, all I care is to work double and feed my family". That my friend is vanity.

Do you know what kind of vanity our LORD wants? It is the "AWARENESS of HIS PRESENCE", in our lives daily. That's a very healthy vanity. So let us be vain about our LORD'S plan for us, to follow His will.

> LORD GOD, thank You for the things I have in my life. May You continue to remind me to be less vain or not to be vain at all. Help me to balance my life, in JESUS' name, I pray Amen!
> 08/05/01

Bible Tidbits

PROMISES CAN BE BROKEN

Matthew 14 : 9 – 10

⁹ The king was distressed, but because of his oaths and the guests who were present, he ordered that it be given, 10 and he had John beheaded in the prison.

It is very honorable to keep one's promise. "Promises are made to be broken", a common saying, but I guess there is truth behind that, if it is for a good cause. King Herod made an oath and for sure he needed to keep it, especially because he was a ruler. But what kind of oath was that? Fulfilling it at the expense of one's life? Worse than that, is the manner it was performed it was brutal and heartless.

Nowadays, we have this procedure called, "mercy killing", in which dying people making their loved ones promise to help them die. There are some people who could do such for money. Think about it. If you have a relative like that, would you promise to help that relative die? Remember we can break the promise, for a good cause. Indeed, we need the Holy Spirit to guide us every step of the way.

LORD GOD, I need You in my life. I can't do anything without You. Please let the Holy Spirit guide me every step of the way, especially when I am faced with the situation like that, "to make or break" a promise. Thank You for the gift of discernment, in JESUS' name I pray Amen!
08/06/01

Esther B. Jimenez

"IT IS I"

Matthew 14 : 27

At once JESUS spoke to them, "Take courage, it is I: do not be afraid."

There is another adage that I would like to share, and it goes like this, "One word is enough for a wise man". I would like to revise it a little bit. How about this, "One Man's Presence is enough for all mankind". Yes, it is Him and no one else is enough reassurance for our welfare. "It is I, do not be afraid", the LORD reassured His disciples.

These three words are very powerful. It is the best reassurance you could ever have. He would take care of us during our life's journey. If you feel insecure at any moment time, just think of those three words, "It is I", and the LORD will let you feel His Presence and your insecurities will disappear. GOD knows us and if we have a little faith, He'll make it grow. All we have to do is to will it.

LORD GOD, thank You for Your reassurances. "It is I", as You said! Yes LORD It is You, so let me leave everything in Your care, my anxieties, my insecurities and my worries. All this I pray in JESUS' name Amen!
08/07/01

WHAT A PRIVILEGE?

Luke 22 : 29 – 30

29 and I confer a kingdom on you, just as my Father has conferred one on me, 30 that you may eat and drink at my table in my kingdom; and you will sit on thrones judging the twelve tribes of Israel.

It would be a great honor, dining with Our LORD. Sometimes, when I read part of the Bible like this scene, with the twelve apostles, I imagine myself as one of the guests. Then I try to feel the atmosphere and the silence. True enough, I could really feel that the LORD is talking to His apostles through their hearts.

Dining with the LORD is not a one time shot. It is a privilege for us to eat and drink with Him, through the liturgy, and it is a long term relationship with our LORD. We are given this privilege not only for our spiritual growth, but for our eternal salvation. So if you want to dine with Our LORD every meal forever, you must know Him and you should have a deeper relationship with Him. The privilege is there, but you have to ask for it. We need spiritual effort to do that and of course the grace of GOD. What a privilege huh?

LORD GOD, allow me to have that privilege and grant me the grace of faithfulness. I would like to eat and drink with You in Your Kingdom. I pray this in JESUS' name Amen!
08/07/01

Esther B. Jimenez

ONE WAY STREET TO PEACE

Baruch 3 : 13

Had you walked in the way of GOD, you would have dwelt in enduring peace.

I never was contented with my life before. I always tell myself, if I do this and do that, I'll be happy, or I'll be contented. I was wrong. I never realized that I have to surrender everything to GOD, and contentment will be there. Yes, I have peace in my heart now, compared to my previous life. Why? There's only one answer. I learned to walk through the way of GOD, the "one way street to peace".

I humbly asked GOD to grant me the grace of peace. When you go to a one way street to peace, you'll be facing a lot of bumpy roads and one of them is learning to forgive. If I didn't do this, I would never have the chance to go on to that one way street to peace. Ponder on this and ask our LORD to grant you this privilege.

LORD GOD, I thank You for the peace and contentment that the Holy Spirit has given me. I know I would be facing more difficulties in life and I pray that You'll give me an awareness, that I should walk with You now and even after, through eternal peace, in JESUS' name, I pray, Amen!
08/07/01

Bible Tidbits

CHILDREN ARE US

Matthew 19 : 13 – 14

13 Then children were brought to Him that He might lay His hands on them and pray. The disciples rebuked them, 14 but JESUS said, "Let the children come to me, and do not prevent them; for the kingdom of heaven belongs to such as these".

There is a store, "Kids R Us", a store "Toys R Us" and a store "Babies' R Us", and you can buy variety of stuff for kids. Children play an important part in this world but most of all in JESUS' life. He cares about them so much and he is fond of them. Imagine Him, smiling and blessing each child. The children are our future; "Children Are Us". Show them your love and care.

Be responsible for their needs. Just think of the reassurances we have, "The Kingdom Of GOD", belongs to them.

Bless your sons and daughters every chance you have. Nurture them, not only physically, but spiritually.

LORD GOD, I have been a child once and I thank You for that opportunity. I could be childlike, trusting everything in Your Hands. Bless the children in our family, the children in the whole world. I pray all this in JESUS' name, Amen!
08/08/01

Esther B. Jimenez

POWERFUL SEED

Matthew 17 : 20

He said to them, "Because of your little faith, Amen I say to you, if you have faith the size of a mustard seed, you will say to this mountain, "Move from here to there and it will move. Nothing will be impossible for you".

I was attending a three day retreat, three years ago and the priest who conducted the retreat gave each of us a small packet with mustard seeds inside.

I did not know what mustard seeds look like, so when I opened the packet I saw very tiny seeds.

A seed is like the size of the dot (.), a period at the end of a sentence. Imagine how small it is and yet GOD looks forward for our faith even as little as this seed. So even though we have this kind of faith, more blessings will come because GOD will take care of its growth.

The mustard seed is indeed a "powerful seed".

LORD GOD, I thank You for the gifts of the Holy Spirit, for granting me the gift of faith. Remind me LORD how powerful it is to have a faith size of a mustard seed. I pray to have my faith grow forever, in JESUS' name, Amen!
08/0/01

BEHIND THE TRUTH

John 8 : 31 – 32

31 JESUS then said to those Jews who believed in Him, If you remain in my word, you will truly be my disciples, 32 and you will know the truth, and the truth will set you free.

Often times we are victims of suppressing our emotions especially anger. If anger piles up, the tendency for us is to burst out. We keep things behind, or keep things to ourselves, to protect the people we love. We, too, love the "white lies", because we don't have the courage to tell the truth. We are uptight because of the guilt feelings we have and the worst part is, these things lead to anxiety and the end result is no peace at all.

So what are we going to do about it? Just turn your head behind you and you will see behind… the truth. And behind the truth is freedom, freedom from fear, freedom from worries and freedom from uncertainties. And peace will come.

Remember, behind The WORD is the Truth and the Truth will set us free.

LORD GOD, thank You for leading me to the right direction and for giving me the gift of discernment. Grant me O LORD, the grace to tell the truth all the time and grant me peace in my heart, in JESUS' name, I pray Amen!
08/09/01

Esther B. Jimenez

GOD IS WITH US

Matthew 1 : 23

"Behold, the virgin shall be with child and bear a son, and they shall name him, Emmanuel", which means "GOD IS WITH US".

Giving names to newly born babies is pretty exciting. You choose a name for a baby from a book of names, sometimes from combining both parents' names or grandparents' names, names not in the book, but you know the meaning, sometimes random names, names of the heroes or heroines, names of the Saints and so forth.

My name means, "Star", Estrella. When I asked my parents where they got my name, they said the meaning is beautiful and that's it. And mind you I like it too. I am glad that, this was the name they chose.

Imagine, if we have one name for everyone and it's Emmanuel, "GOD IS WITH US", for sure we'll be aware that GOD is everywhere. There is a very essential reason why that beautiful name was given… that is to remind us that GOD is in everyone's heart. It is the Name above all names.

LORD GOD, thank You for the meaning of Emmanuel. It is not only a symbolic name, but You are with us every moment. May You continue to bless us and guide us. May Your name be in our hearts all the time, in JESUS' name, I pray Amen!
08/10/01

Bible Tidbits

SHEEP'S GATE

John 10 : 7 & 9

7 So JESUS said again, "Amen, amen I say to you, I am the gate for the sheep. 9 I am the gate. Whoever enters through me will be saved, and will come in and go out and find pasture.

I am wondering and pondering on these verses and I would love to be one of the sheep in the Bible. It's a great opportunity to pass that gate, the gate that will save me. We are not aware at this time that we can have that kind of opportunity, to pass through the sheep's gate. The passport to go through that gate is, "transformation". This gate is not an ordinary gate. It is the gate to salvation. This Gate is the One Who promised salvation for all mankind. So what are we waiting for? Let us work our way to the extraordinary, super, sturdy gate, and let us show our passport to transformation.

LORD GOD, thank You for being our Sheep Gate, our Shepherd as well. You're not only pasturing us, but Your gate is totally open for us. Thank You for allowing us to enter through that special gate. Grant us LORD, the grace of transformation, our passport to Your precious gate, the gate to salvation. I pray all this in JESUS' name, Amen!
08/10/01

Esther B. Jimenez

GENEROSITY

2 Corinthians 9 : 6 – 7

**6 Consider this: whoever sows sparingly will also reap sparingly and whoever sows bountifully will reap bountifully.
7 Each must do as already determined, without sadness or compulsion, for GOD loves a cheerful giver.**

My nephew was with me one Sunday noon at the church. During collection, I saw him putting $5.00 in the basket. After the mass, I asked him why he gave his allowance. He told me, "I want to give more, Auntie, but I don't have enough. GOD gives me a lot and everything comes from Him". What a beautiful virtue of generosity, especially coming from a kid. It's not the amount, it's not the number of times, it is the depth of your heart that counts in giving.

When I hear somebody say, "I always give from the bottom of my heart", I just ponder for a moment and think how deep is the bottom of that heart ?

It is literally said, but the translation denotes sincerity and generosity. So remember, GOD knows our hearts and He loves a cheerful giver.

LORD GOD, I thank You for the gift of generosity. Thank You for touching the children's hearts, including my nephew's. Let me think of others LORD, when I am receiving Your abundance. Grant me LORD the gift of service so I can serve You the way You wanted to be served. I pray this in JESUS' name, Amen!
08/11/01

Bible Tidbits

LOSING IS GAINING

Philippians 3 : 7 – 8

7 (But) whatever gains I had, these I have come to consider a loss because of CHRIST. 8 More than that, I even consider everything as a loss because of the supreme good of knowing CHRIST JESUS my LORD....

This is somewhat paradoxical. How can you gain when you're losing? You see, if you know JESUS, and have a deeper relationship with Him, you won't even care about the wealth and the fame around you. He will give you contentment and peace. So don't be afraid to pray, or even say you surrender everything to Him and mean it as well. You lose yourself but you gain Him.

The advantage of losing your materialism is gaining points for a better relationship with JESUS, and you are investing your points for the heavenly kingdom.

The key here is "knowing our LORD JESUS CHRIST". To know Him is to serve Him the way He wanted to be served. But you have to have a willing heart.

This is what I call "the victory of losing", "gaining the trophy of salvation".

LORD GOD, I would like to pray the prayer that I got from the missal book in our church.

"Dedication To JESUS".
LORD JESUS CHRIST, take all my memory, my understanding and my will. All that I have and cherish, you have given me; I surrender it all to be guided by Your will. Your love and Your grace are wealth enough for me. Give me these LORD JESUS and I ask for nothing more. Amen!
(From St. Ignatius Loyola 1491-1556)
08/11/01

Esther B. Jimenez

THE BEST ADVERTISING

Deuteronomy 6 : 4 – 5

**4 "Hear, O Israel! The LORD is our GOD, the LORD alone!
5 Therefore you shall love the LORD, your GOD, with all your heart, and with all your soul, and with all your strength".**

They say that the best advertising is by word of mouth. This was what Moses did. He shouted to the people of Israel on how to love the LORD, and even how to do it.

It was a very clear form of advertising because the messages were specified.

I have been an advertising sales representative and if this is the kind of message to impart to the consumers, I will have a lot of clients who will patronize my advertisers. If you believe in any advertising today, you must also believe in Moses' messages. The spreading of the Good News and the fulfillment of the prophets' visions are the best advertising.

Another thing is listening to the Gospel Readings at the Masses and of course the homilies are effective advertising. When you talk about GOD's greatness, kindness and goodness, that is the best advertising.

Continue to read the verses 6 – 9 and you'll know more how Moses reinforced the messages of GOD.

> LORD GOD, we patronize a lot of different products. But, what we need are effective products that are strong, meaningful and products that last, and LORD, Your Word is the best. So my LORD, may You guide me in my everyday use of advertising, (the Christian messages). I pray all this in JESUS' name, Amen!
> 08/11/01

THE ESSENCE OF FAITH

Hebrews 11 : 1

Faith is the realization of what is hoped for and evidence of things not seen.

There is a popular adage that says, "to see is to believe". It is very clear that there is no sign of faith in this adage. To believe but have not seen, is genuine faith. In our daily lives, faith is always at the back of the picture. We always do a test to prove things; we think we are successful because of our own effort. We do things our way even it is not righteous. We do things because we don't know the essence of faith, the faith that should keep us going.

If you want to know the real essence of faith, I recommend that you read the Profession of Faith in the Catechism of the Catholic Church and ponder on it.

Remember the story of Thomas? He didn't believe that JESUS CHRIST was resurrected. He even demanded to touch our LORD's body to find out for himself if He was the One whom He said He was. How about You? Do you go for, "to see is to believe??? Or believe, but you haven't seen???"

> LORD GOD, thank You for the gift of faith, knowing You are there all the time and that we should surrender everything in Your Hand. I pray that You will continue to grant me the faith that I need, to go on in serving You, in JESUS' name. Amen!
> 08/11/01

Esther B. Jimenez

FREE CHOICE

Sirach 15 : 14 – 15

14 When GOD, in the beginning, created man, he made him subject to his own free choice. 15 If you choose, you can keep the commandments; it is loyalty to do his will.

We are living in this world with balances to weigh. We have up or down; open or close; left or right: black or white; hot or cold: run or walk; go or stop; and many more. We have a lot of choices in between. But the most critical choice we are facing is, to do good or to do evil.

Often times we blame GOD for our misfortunes, for our fates, and even for our choices. We are accountable for every action we do. GOD gives us the freedom to choose. And only GOD can grant the grace to do His will. We have this freedom, so choose life instead of death. Just remember, we die on earth to be born again in heaven, to experience the eternal life with Him.

It is one of the greatest privileges we have in life, the freedom of choice.

So what are you going to choose?

LORD GOD, thank You for the gift of life, the freedom to choose and all the graces that You have given me. I ask You LORD that in every discernment I make, You'll be there to help me, In JESUS' name, I pray, Amen!
08/11/01

Bible Tidbits

MEDITATION VS. REFLECTION

Sirach 14 : 20

Happy the man who meditates on wisdom, and reflects on knowledge.

    I have been reading the lives of the saints lately, and I came to realize that they were ordinary people who did extraordinary things. Most of them were victims of persecution and some of them died martyrs. They were happy handling their lives, because they lived in prayers, in meditation, contemplation, pondering the Word of GOD; and reflecting the messages they received from our LORD. In other words the wisdom they had, came from GOD and that made them live in joy and peace. Everyone has the potential to be a saint.

    Do you know what motivates me to be holy? I look forward to being a saint someday. And that's why I ask for more graces to go on with my transformation. So let's work with our prayers, our meditation and reflection.

    Be happy, be holy and use the knowledge that you have wisely and divinely.

    LORD GOD, thank You for the gifts of the Holy Spirit that You have given me, especially the gift of wisdom and the gift of knowledge. Indeed I am happy writing these reflections and I thank the Holy Spirit for all His leads. I pray everything in JESUS' name, Amen!
08/11/01

Esther B. Jimenez

HANDMAIDS OF THE LORD

Luke 1 : 46 – 48

46 And Mary said, "My soul proclaims the greatness of the LORD; 47 my spirit rejoices in GOD my Savior. 48 For He Has looked upon His handmaid's lowliness; behold, from now on will all ages call me blessed.

I encourage the readers to ponder on these verses 46-55, about the Canticle of Mary, especially to all women, single, widow or married, with or without children, young or old.

What an inspiration for us women, to just imitate Mary's virtues, especially as a mother. We can all be handmaids of the LORD. Mary is a faithful, humble, obedient woman and a model of perfection. Let us live with Mary's virtues and surely we are protected by GOD's promise, the promise of love and mercy.

LORD GOD, I thank You for Your Mother, for giving birth to Your Son, through the Holy Spirit. Thank You for her gift of intercession. LORD, I would like to offer part of my poem, that I wrote for Our Blessed Virgin Mary.
We clasp our hands and bow down to You,
To show our profound reverence,
We are glad to have you as our mother,
Our Lady, thank You for having Our JESUS.
We honor and respect you Our Mother,
You are our model of perfection,
You are a virgin and a true martyr,
Our Lady, help us in our transformation.
I pray everything in JESUS' name, Amen!
08/11/01

MARCH WITH GOD

Deuteronomy 31 : 6

Be brave and steadfast; have no fear or dread of them, for it is the LORD, Your GOD, who marches with you; he will never fail you or forsake you.

I honor all soldiers who fought for their country. Whether they were driven by parents, or influenced by friends or brought along by unavoidable circumstances, they still have brave hearts. I salute them and admire them..

We who are not soldiers constantly are also in a war, like spiritual warfare, family feud, or any unexpected battle. But now and then, we are reassured that our LORD marches with us. He will protect us and He will give us spiritual aid. We have to be humble to let Him know that we need him. So from now on, let us march with GOD, with a steadfast and brave heart. We can be soldiers too, fighting a good fight, combating the abominations here on earth. Our LORD never abandons us nor forsakes us. We have to trust Him if You want to march with Him. So let's go forward, march!!!

LORD GOD, I thank You for the spiritual strength that You have given me; for marching with me in my spiritual struggle. I pray everything in JESUS' name, Amen!
08/12/01

I have written a short prayer-poem for all soldiers.

Esther B. Jimenez

SOLDIERS' PRAYER

LORD, we are here in the midst of a battle,
Defending the country we stand for,
We are with our brothers and sisters in uniform,
To fight and serve as we vow to hold on.
No one knows when this war will end,
But we have to leave everything in Your Hands,
So, please guide us every step of the way,
Protect our families and loved ones as well;
We pray this in JESUS name, Amen!

Bible Tidbits

FORGIVE, HOW MANY TIMES?

Matthew 18 : 21 - 22

**21 Then Peter approaching asked Him, "LORD, if my brother sins against me, how often must I forgive him? As many as seven times?
22 JESUS answered, "I say to you, not seven times but seventy-seven times.**

We human beings have difficulty in forgiving and not only that, we just don't forget. We dwell on the hurts and the heartaches, then it takes us a long time to forget them. It lingers almost forever.

Pride is in the way of forgiveness. Forgiveness is difficult, yes it is, but if we can learn to forgive a number of times, then the chance to be humble is also limitless. So don't limit your forgiveness to just one time. You still have seventy-six times.

Actually, forgiving without forgetting is as good as not forgiving at all. Again, "It is not possible", you may say; but with GOD'S grace, and you must ask for it, everything will be in the proper place. He will help you to forgive and to forget. So learn to forgive and to forget and you'll earn your peace. Again, how many times???????

> LORD GOD, allow me to ask for Your forgiveness. I thank You for Your never-ending love and mercy. Please, grant me LORD the grace of forgiveness. Let me forgive those who have hurt me. And may I be forgiven for hurting my loved ones, even the people that I hurt unknowingly. LORD have mercy, CHRIST have mercy and LORD, have mercy, in JESUS' name I pray, Amen!
> 08/12/01

LOVE COUNTS

1 Corinthians 13 : 2

And if I have the gift of prophesy and comprehend all mysteries and all knowledge; if I have all faith so as to move mountains, but do not have love, I am nothing.

Love is a powerful word, a great virtue and an important aspect of any relationship. Let us not take for granted the value and essence of love. Now, let us dig into the real meaning of love. Love is not to be ignored. A simple life, full of love lasts forever. Love is indeed extended beyond this earth. Remember, love counts. We don't want to be nothing in this world and the only way to be somebody in GOD's sight is to have an honest and sincere love.

When GOD created mankind, he created us with love. He has shown His love in many mysterious ways, and even to the extent of sending His Son to redeem us. Love counts indeed and it plays a huge role in this world. It's mentioned in the Bible, both in the Old Testament and in the New Testament many, many times. Again, Love counts.

LORD GOD, You have shown Your love and have extended Your mercy. I thank You for letting me know that love counts, wherever I go and whatever I do. I thank You for allowing me to love and be loved, I pray this in JESUS' name, Amen!
08/13/01

THE FAITHFUL ONE

2 Thessalonians 3 : 3

But the LORD is faithful: he will strengthen you and guard you from the evil one.

Every time I hear or read the word, "faithful" the following words always come into my mind; "through thick and thin", "rain or shine", and "come what may".

These are strong words that seem unbreakable or inseparable. This is also a description of an everlasting compact between two people or two parties.

GOD loves us through thick and thin; He guides us rain or shine; He is there come what may, regardless of how much we hurt Him. We have a forgiving GOD that showers us with an unconditional love.

He is the most Faithful One. Can we be that faithful, too? Can we show our love and commitment too?

It is a great feeling to know that there is Someone Who is very sincere and faithful to us.

LORD GOD, I thank You for Your faithfulness, for Your guidance and protection. I ask that You grant me the gift of faithfulness. Forgive me, LORD, for sometimes I ignore Your loyalty to me. May You continue to be faithful to us, in JESUS' name, I pray, Amen!
08/13/01

Esther B. Jimenez

ACTION SPEAKS THE TRUTH

1 John 3 : 18

Children, let us love not in word or speech but in deed and truth.

There is an adage that says, "action speaks louder than words". Are we talking about body language here? In a way, yes, because when you put your thoughts into acts you have to move your body. You can tell people that you love them but without showing them, the message of love won't be received. Giving a hand to your life partner, offering your service to the community, being generous to the needy or having ears to be willing to listen attentively, hugging someone in grief, patting somebody on the back who did a good job, smiling all the time are actions and gestures of love. I can go on and on, but the point here is, love should be incorporated with action. And of course, when you say something pleasant, be it a greeting or a compliment or advice, be truthful and be sincere.

I admire those politicians who are implementing what they say into actions. So, from now on, prove to someone that you love them by your thoughtful actions, and by your gentle approach. Remember, "action speaks the truth".

> LORD GOD, thank You for Your message about love and what does it entails. I ask that You may guide my actions, guard my thoughts, tame my tongue and give me holy ears, to listen and extend my help. I pray this in JESUS' name Amen!
> 08/13/01

PROPER ENDORSEMENT

John 14 : 16

And I will ask the Father, and He will give another Advocate to be with you always.

GOD gave His Son for us to redeem us, to ransom us, to save us from our sin. JESUS CHRIST became man to let us know how much He loves us through His redemptive suffering.

Many of us do not realize that in our daily lives, we have a constant companion, the Holy Spirit, the Advocate, the Counselor. When Our LORD JESUS left us and promised to come back, He made a proper endorsement, that is to have our Advocate to be with us constantly.

I rely for everything from my constant Companion. I entrust all my plans and decisions on the gifts of the Holy Spirit that I received. You see, this Advocate is not only to watch us, but to give us a lot of gifts. But you should have the willingness to accept those gifts. That's how Our LORD loves us. He is making sure that we are taken cared of. He will not abandon us, that's why there is a proper endorsement. So, will you acknowledge this wonderful endorsement? Are you ready to open the gifts that you already have?

Are you going to make your decisions by depending on Your Advocate?

LORD GOD, thank You for the proper endorsement, and for our constant Companion, the Advocate. LORD, even though I can't see You, I could feel You in my heart, and in my whole being. You are the Spirit of truth. I pray everything in JESUS' name in the unity of the Holy Spirit, one GOD forever and ever, Amen!
08/14/01

Esther B. Jimenez

THE MAP OF LIFE

Jeremiah 29 : 11

For I know well the plans I have in mind for you, says the LORD, plans for your welfare, not for woe! plans to give you a future full of hope.

Each one of us has a blueprint of the map of our lives. As soon as we wake up in the morning, we do our routines such as: preparing for work, going to the grocery after work, or going to a friend's house, or dining with someone or bringing the kids to the shopping mall, etc.

We plan for our future, setting up our goals, working hard for better accomplishments and achievements. Then all of a sudden we are faced with a calamity, problems of all sorts, troubles about kids, family feuds, work clashes and many more.

These plans of ours are subject to change every moment because GOD has different plans for us, and definitely for our welfare and for our betterment. Just remember to ask GOD's guidance for any of your plans, and you'll see that His plans work better than ours. So, follow your map of life's blueprint, the blueprint made for heaven.

LORD GOD, it is very clear what the prophet Jeremiah said about Your plans for us. I thank You for the map of my life, my blueprint to holiness, towards Your kingdom. Please continue to clear my pathway, LORD. I pray this in JESUS' name, Amen!
08/14/01

WILLINGNESS

Isaiah 6 : 8

Then I heard the voice of the LORD saying, "Whom shall I send? Who will go for us?" "Here I am." I said: "send me!"

Again, I would like to mention how I admired those soldiers who fought for their countries. They enlisted themselves for a good cause. Serving the community church, or volunteering to render service to any group or institution is rewarding.

Willingness is a great virtue, especially if it's a sign of GOD's call. I know that some people don't have time to do extra things, but I strongly believe that going an extra mile, will be extra rewarding. Have you thought about going an extra mile?

I feel fulfilled every time I am scheduled to serve as a Eucharistic Minister. I am honored to hold the Body of CHRIST and the Cup of His Blood. I also volunteered to say a group rosary with the residents in the nursing home. Willingness of the heart is the key to service. If you run across an opportunity to serve voluntarily, will you grab that chance? Will you say, "LORD, here I am".

LORD GOD, here I am, to serve You. Allow me to serve You, the way You want to be served. Grant me LORD, the gift of willingness and the grace of humility, in JESUS' name I pray, in the unity of the Holy Spirit one GOD forever and ever, Amen!
08/14/01

Esther B. Jimenez

CHALLENGES IN LIFE

James 1 : 2 – 3

**2 Consider it all joy, my brothers, when you encounter various trials,
3 for you know that the testing of your faith produces perseverance.**

Life is full of challenges, and that makes life interesting and
exciting. They say that, "all work and no play makes a person a dull person". So, a workaholic person is living a dull and boring life? Excessive work is not exciting and challenging. Changing is challenging.

The way I look at life is, you can turn your trials into triumphs… triumphs of joy. But you can only attain this, through GOD's grace, especially the grace of faith. GOD is so generous in giving us a lot of graces and gifts through the Holy Spirit. And these graces and gifts lead from one virtue to another virtue. Just wait and see, and you will experience the holy connection of trials with happiness. Let us be open to the Holy Spirit. Now, we can start unwrapping our gifts that we already have.

LORD GOD, thank You for the gifts and graces that You have given me, and the virtues that I use in my daily life. Thank You for the trials and tribulations, that I learn to lean on You. Let me experience the joy of perseverance LORD, and continue to increase my faith, in JESUS 'name I pray, Amen!
08/15/01

OUR COMPASS TO ETERNAL LIFE

2 Peter 1 : 11

For, in this way, entry into the eternal kingdom of our LORD and Savior JESUS CHRIST will be richly provided for you.

    Boys scouts, girls scouts, soldiers, forest rangers, use a compass to know where they are, and to know where they are going. Even in driving, if we have a compass, it will point out the direction, whether north or south, east or west.

    Do you think we need a compass to the eternal kingdom? What we need is a holy life, a transformed life, and a conversion of our lives. These will guarantee our entry to the eternal kingdom. These will be the compass to the eternal life. We can only attain this holy compass through GOD's grace. So if you are in the middle of nowhere start using the compass to eternal life, such as "holiness, transformation and conversion".

> LORD GOD, I know You have promised us of eternal life and thank You for that promise. Thank You for the reassurances, of that awaiting eternal kingdom. Thank You for the transformation, spiritual strength and spiritual growth. LORD, continue to guide me to Your kingdom, in JESUS' name I pray Amen!
> 08/15/01

THE LORD'S DAY

Hebrews 4:4

For he has spoken somewhere about the seventh day on this manner. And GOD rested on the seventh day from all His works:

In this letter to the Hebrews, it mentioned the word, "somewhere" and to help you where that somewhere is, it's found in Genesis 2 : 3; (So GOD blessed the seventh day and made it holy, because on it, He rested from all work He had done in creation).

There are 365 days in a year, 12 months in a year, 4 weeks in one month, 7 days in a week, why not spare Sunday to worship GOD? Why can't we spend our Sundays to give respect and to honor our LORD on this day, the LORD'S Day? If we can only do that, GOD would be glad and thrilled. Remember, He blessed the seventh day, and indeed His blessings are never-ending ones. I honor the people who go to church everyday. These faithful people are not only praying for themselves. They are interceding for all of us. So let us honor and respect this wonderful day, the day for the LORD, the LORD'S Day.

LORD GOD, I thank You for the chances You have given me, in going to church to attend the mass daily. I pray that You may touch every being, may You give them the gift of obedience to go to church on Sundays and to bring all their family members. I pray too, for the elders that I see daily in the church. I thank You for my family for they spend a day with You, on the LORD'S Day. I pray all this in JESUS' name Amen!
08/15/01

REAR VIEW MIRROR

Philippians 3 : 13

Brothers, I for my part do not consider myself to have taken possession, Just one thing: forgetting what lies behind but straining forward to what lies ahead.

Our lives can be compared to a rear view mirror. Just imagine, when you're driving, you're also looking at the rear view mirror and you only glance once in a while. If you look continuously at your rear view mirror, and not looking where you're heading, you'll meet Mr. Accident and you'll crash your car.

You need your rear view mirror only for viewing and not for focusing.

The same way in our lives; we have to focus on what's coming and not what's behind us. Dwelling on the past is not going to do us any good. If you keep looking and lingering on the thoughts of how miserable you were, you'll end up having more miseries. Look ahead! Enjoy life, it is one of the best gifts we have. We can only live one day at a time.

LORD GOD, help me to focus my mind and heart for the continuance of my transformation. If I dwell on the past, remind me LORD to go on with my life and let me feel Your Presence all the time. I want to be a good driver, so LORD, let me just glance at my rear view mirror. Thank You for helping me to live one day at a time. I pray all this in JESUS' name Amen!
08/15/01

Esther B. Jimenez

THE LIGHT OF OUR LIVES

1 John 1 : 5

Now this is the message that we have heard from Him and proclaim to you: GOD is light, and in Him there is no darkness at all.

What a great reassurance to know that with GOD there is no darkness at all. Believe it, because this is true. No matter how big your problems are, GOD is greater than all those problems. He will show you how to handle your problems, but you have to trust Him and you must have faith. He will help you carry your burdens, your sorrows, your trials and your tribulations. He will show you the light, for He is Light.

So if you're in darkness, if you feel it's dark around you, switch on your everyday light, the light of your life, the light of our lives. Call on Him, our LORD, our Light. Remember this: you can only appreciate the stars and the moon in the dark. Same as our LORD, it is a great relief to know that during our moments of darkness, there He is, in brilliance and radiance, the True Light.

> LORD GOD, GOD of my life; Light of my life, thank You for being there in times of my dark moments. Thank You for being my light. Show me the way LORD, to the spiritual pathway, in JESUS' name I pray Amen!
> 08/16/01

DISCIPLINE

Hebrews 12 : 7

Endure your trials as "discipline", GOD treats you as sons. For what "son" is there whom his father does not discipline?

Discipline is an antidote for bad habits, such as procrastination, addiction, obsession and many more. It is difficult to practice self-discipline. We need the grace of GOD to do this.

The worst part of trying to discipline oneself is falling back and maintaining it. Just like trying to lose weight. The best goal of discipline is…disciplining ourselves not to sin. Again, we can do this through GOD's grace. It is a great feeling, if we can survive the trials and temptations in our lives. And self-discipline aids us in overcoming such. So, again we have to ask for the gift of endurance and self-control. GOD disciplines us through His Laws and Commandments, but He offers us His love and mercy.

> LORD GOD, Heavenly Father, I really need Your help for a lot of things, that need disciplining in my life. I can't do it without Your grace. Grant me LORD, the gift of endurance, spiritual tenacity and self-control. I surrender all my bad habits, my attachments, vanities and obsessions to You. May You bless my daily endeavors. LORD, I pray this in JESUS name Amen!
> 08/16/01

(A stanza from my poem entitled, "Discipline")

You can discipline yourself step by step,
The awaiting reward is indeed great,
If we can discipline ourselves to the fullest
We'll have a happy life and spiritual fitness.

Esther B. Jimenez

BETWEEN ALPHABET LETTERS

Psalm 24 : 1

The earth is the LORD'S and all it holds, the world and those who live there.

I love to journal my reflections on Scriptural passages, my thoughts on certain things, my daily encounters, my prayers and most of all the wisdom that the Holy Spirit prompts me to write.

So whenever the Holy Spirit leads me, I follow. Like this morning while I was fishing, a wisdom came in to my thoughts. I do not know if you have already encountered the things I am going to share. But I still would like to share it. Who knows, it might be a reminder.

Let us analyze the word, "world". GOD created the world and He owns us. A lot of times, we are focused more on the "world". So when you start feeling it's too much of a world for you, all you have to do is…hold on the "L",(from the word, "world") and what is left is GOD's Word. And that "L" is the LORD. Try it! Hold on to the LORD'S Word until it separates from the world.

So read not only between lines, but between alphabet letters.

LORD GOD, sometimes Your messages are just in between alphabet letters. I thank You for Your holy wisdom and I pray that You may continue to give me messages. LORD, grant me the gift of generosity that I may be able to share to other people. I'll hold on You LORD and Your Word will be my guide in this world. I pray all this in JESUS' name Amen!
08/16/01

Bible Tidbits

HUNGER AND THIRST

John 6 : 35

JESUS said to them, "I am the bread of life"; whoever comes to me will never hunger, and whoever believes in me will never thirst.

Hunger is a terrible feeling. Thirst is the same. We crave to eat and we crave to drink, so we can fill our needs, respectively. Imagine, not to be hungry and not to be thirsty forever. We can only attain this with GOD's grace. If you are hungry for knowledge about GOD, you are on the right track. Knowing GOD is to join Him during meals. He is our Bread of Life and Soul Quencher. Believe in His words and trust Him. We will remain full, as long as we follow His laws. He will fill up our hunger and thirst. Just wait and watch for the gifts of the Holy Spirit and be open, for these gifts will aid you in your hunger and thirst. Ask GOD for the grace of faith, and this will be the start of your appetite in knowing Him more.

LORD GOD, I thirst for you. I pray that You'll always quench my thirst. I know I'll never be hungry and thirsty, as long as I am faithful to Your commandments. Thank You for the fullness of my heart and thank You for allowing me to crave for you. I pray for our spiritual abundance, in JESUS' name Amen!
8/16/01

Esther B. Jimenez

PASS OR FAIL

2 Corinthians 13 : 5

Examine yourselves to see whether you are living in faith. Test yourselves. Do you not realize that JESUS CHRIST is in you?- unless, of course, you fail the test.

We have been through a lot of tests; academic tests, entrance exams, physical tests, board exams, etc. There is a passing grade and a failing grade and there is a standard measurement to meet. This is the same as, whether JESUS is in us or not. One very important thing to consider in this kind of test is… the preparation before confession. The Catholic Church has ways for us to examine our conscience, to guide the people who go to confession. This counts a lot, because this will detect if you are living in faith.

You know it's a great feeling to have confessed your wrong doings. There is peace in your heart. I know this because that's what I feel every time I go to confession. Peace is the reward and it is a sign of a passing grade. We have to imitate JESUS and we must see JESUS in everyone's face.

Remember, we have a forgiving GOD. We don't want to fail, do we?

Let me repeat the question in the Scripture, "Do you not realize that JESUS CHRIST is in you?

LORD GOD, I would like to pass with flying colors. The only way to attain this is to just be aware that You are there all the time to guide my thoughts and my conscience. Help me to examine my conscience and help me LORD to repent for all my sins, In JESUS' name I pray, Amen!
08/16/01

Bible Tidbits

INCENTIVE

James 5 : 20

….* he should know that whoever brings back a sinner from the error of his way will save his soul from death and will cover a multitude of sins.

In the business world, like in big companies or even small companies, they always have something to promote. They spend tons of money in advertising, with lots of incentives for the perspective buyers. You'll see some of their promotions as, "Buy one take one", or "50% off", or "Bring your coupon for free installation", etc. It is pretty tempting at times to go for promotional advertising. What an incentive, huh?

The message from James is really rewarding. It is the best incentive I've ever known and the most productive, too. Imagine if we can save someone from committing a sin, if we can talk to somebody to get out of his/her crooked life, or if we can be a good listener for someone in distress, or someone with suicidal thoughts; or simply tell someone that believing in the horoscope is a venial sin. If we can do all these things for them, we will be given more blessings and we'll be given a very lucrative incentive. It also applies to someone who could do the same thing for us. But in order to do these, we should be living the Word of GOD too, and we should ask His grace to do His will.

So let us work together in saving each other to cover a multitude of sins.

LORD GOD, I humbly surrender and confess to You all my sins. Again, thank You for my conversion. Grant me LORD, the gift of righteousness and prudence. Make me humble in a spiritual way, not in spiritual pride. I ask this in JESUS' name, Amen!
08/17/01

Esther B. Jimenez

CELIBACY

Matthew 19 : 12

Some are incapable of marriage because they were born so; some, because they were made so by others; some, because they have renounced marriage for the sake of the kingdom of heaven. Whoever can accept this ought to accept it.

According to Mr. Webster, "celibacy" is the state of being not married; abstention from sexual intercourse; abstention by vow from marriage. It is very clear what Scriptures are saying about the different categories or descriptions of marital life. Sex is a beautiful thing and even in the beginning GOD created a perfect couple before the original sin happened. But the most beautiful thing is how you handle your marital life, and the consequences that are included in marriage. Whatever state of marital life you are in, "respect for each other", must be kept in mind. For those who are celibates, I honor them, for renouncing sex for the sake of GOD's reign. I have high regards for widows and widowers who never married after their spouses died, especially those who spent their time in the church or serving in their communities.

LORD GOD, thank You for the clear messages, of what the Scriptures say regarding marital status. Thank You for the spiritual insights. Thank You LORD for the life of celibacy. Thank You LORD, for this gift of celibacy that You have given me. Thank You for allowing me to feel good of who I am. You are an understanding GOD and I love You and bless You, too LORD, in JESUS name I pray, Amen!
08/17/01

POOR VS. RICH

Luke 6 : 20

And raising his eyes toward his disciples he said: "Blessed are you who are poor, for the kingdom of GOD is yours.

These beatitudes in the gospel of Luke are indeed paradoxical. There are some people who are rich and wealthy, that don't like to be poor. Maybe they think they owed their fame to themselves. Nothing is wrong in being rich and famous, but that is not what the Scriptures said. The poor are blessed too, same as the rich. But the difference is the kingdom of GOD will be for the poor.

There are many "squatters" in our country, the Philippines. And these "squatters" are the poor people. But when you visit them, they seem to be happy, no signs of stress. They eat simple meals daily, kids play, mothers wash their clothes, and fathers chop wood to use for cooking. This is a true picture of a poor family. There are lots of poor families and indigent people all over the world.

Beatitudes are worth reading and worth pondering. These are the keys to humility. Luke is inviting you to read and ponder on the beatitudes.

LORD GOD, thank You for blessing all people who are victims of poverty; for touching their lives; for your reassurances of heavenly kingdom and for the peace and contentment. Thank You also LORD, for the rich people who have generous hearts. Please continue to give your love and mercy on all of us. I personally would like to thank You for allowing me to pray for them, thank You for the gift of intercession, In JESUS' name' I pray Amen!
08/17/01

Esther B. Jimenez

THE WAY TO SAINTHOOD

Romans 12 : 21

Do not be conquered by evil but conquer evil with good.

A lot of things I learned from the moment my life has been transformed. One great lesson is, no turning back whatever the turning point is.

Another lesson is, it's easier to do bad things than to do good things, and the only way to accomplish the latter is through GOD's grace. Persecution is the cause of one soul's downfall. But people who are victims of persecution and other predicaments are in a spiritual warfare situation. The positive side of persecution is, it will aid you to be stronger, that is if you really ask GOD's grace, especially the grace of prudence and self-control. One of the martyrs that I can think of is Maximillian Kolbe. He conquered evil through a good deed, by taking the place of a fellow prisoner, who was about to be executed by the ill-mannered soldiers. There were many more Saints who had encountered evil in their times, and they were able to conquer those evil by their constant asking of grace from GOD. They were very good in casting evil whispers and they were guided by the Holy Spirit, and prompted to say, "In the Name of JESUS I cast you out demon". So we can also conquer evil whispers through casting them out, "In the Name of JESUS".

It will take a lot of GOD's gifts and graces to be holy and to be a saint, but we can start..

> LORD GOD, many times I read and heard about sainthood, that everyone is called to be a saint. I would like to be one. Grant me LORD the grace to rebuke temptations all the time and to stand for the righteous deeds. Make me holier today than yesterday, and holier tomorrow than today. I pray this in JESUS' name Amen!
> 08/17/01

THE SOURCE

2 Corinthians 3 : 5

Not that of ourselves we are qualified to take credit for anything as coming from us: rather, our qualification comes from GOD.

It is very clear in Jeremiah 29:11, that GOD has plans for everyone. GOD knows where we are going, and what we are going to be.

We owe our success to Him and sometimes we take credit for the things we attain and for the things we accomplish in life. He pre-qualifies each of us. GOD takes care of our resumes and our interviews. The job we have comes from Him; the success of the business still comes from Him. The wisdom we have, the promotion we attain and everything no doubt comes from His power. Whether we admit it or not, He is the only Source. He is also the Source of healing. He is the Source of everything.

> LORD GOD, thank You for the education I have. I wouldn't be in this stage of life, if not for You. You are the only One LORD, that did all these. My success is You. Without You I am nothing. Grant me LORD the gift of humility and honesty. Thank You for the gift of life, the Source of life. I pray this in JESUS' name Amen!
> 08/17/01

Esther B. Jimenez

SANCTUARY

Joshua 24 : 26 -27

… 26… Then he took a large stone and set it up there under the oak that was in the sanctuary of the LORD. 27…And Joshua said to all people, "This stone shall be our witness, for it has heard all the words which the LORD spoke to us. It shall be a witness against you, should you wish to deny your GOD.

Now, let's see what a sanctuary is? It is a holy place; also a place where you can find peace, and can commune with the Almighty and also a place for meditation.

For me, nature strikes me as a peaceful surrounding, such as the sea, the forest, the pond, the river, the lake and even the mountainside.

I love fishing and I do my fishing at a small lake, 5 minutes away from my house.

I feel the peace in my heart and I always witness the sunrise and the sunset. The water, the trees, the breeze, the sun, and the rain and my small prayerbook are my witnesses in my conversation with GOD; just like the stone in Joshua's time.

I have a few more sanctuaries that I go to, like spending a few hours in front of the Blessed Sacrament. The thing that counts is, JESUS must be in our hearts all the time. And wherever we are, He is there because He is the Best Sanctuary.

LORD GOD, thank You for all Your creations and creatures, the man-made sanctuaries like the churches and temples. You are in my heart LORD all the time. You are my Sanctuary and thank You for that grace in JESUS' name I pray Amen!
08/18/01

ROAD TO SALVATION

Matthew 19 : 21

JESUS said to him, "If you wish to be perfect, go, sell what you have and give to the poor, and you will have treasure in heaven. Then come, follow me.

How can you just sell your possessions and just give them to the poor? It's not easy. Right? Wrong! Always remember we are only temporarily in this world. Yes, it is difficult to surrender the wealth that you worked hard for. But we can't take our treasure with us when we die. Eternal Kingdom, (the everlasting life) is greater than any wealth. You can put all the wealth together in this world, still it's nothing, compared with the reward that is ahead of us. Aren't you curious about what heaven looks like? And what treasure you will see in that place?

Live a simple life; always be ready; walk light in every flight and possess nothing and most of all work on your road to salvation.

LORD GOD, thank You for the realization that we have to surrender everything to You, including our material needs. I thank You for the wealth that I possess. You are my Wealth, LORD. Grant me LORD, the grace of humility, in JESUS' name, I pray, Amen!
08/18/01

Esther B. Jimenez

TAME YOUR TONGUE

James 3 : 6

The tongue is also a fire. It exists among our member as a world of malice, defiling the whole body and setting the entire course of our lives on fire, itself set on fire by Gehenna.

The tongue is so powerful. It could cut you through hurting words, or it could lift you up through compliments or praises.

There is a saying that says, "If you have nothing good to say, just keep your mouth shut". Bite your tongue if you're tempted to say something bad. The tongue can cause a big fire, or it can prevent the fire, before it spreads. It can tell a lie or can tell the truth.

So you have the choice to let your tongue be burned or tamed. In order to tame your tongue, you have to ask GOD's grace first. Always think twice or more, before you speak or open your mouth. Do not stick with the people who love to gossip. Use your tongue wisely and divinely.

LORD GOD, thank You for I am able to speak and express what I want to say. Grant me LORD, the grace of self-control. Tame my tongue and guard my thoughts. May You always guide my dialogue with others, that I may not say something unpleasant, that I may use my tongue to compliment people and to praise You all the time. I pray this in JESUS' name Amen!
08/19/01

Bible Tidbits

IN JESUS NAME

Colossians 3 : 17

And whatever you do, in word, or in deed, do everything in the name of JESUS, giving thanks to GOD the Father through Him.

We need to be reminded all the time that GOD sent His Son JESUS to save us; to redeem us. And that's GOD'S plan of salvation for mankind.

Some of us don't have the realization yet about how deep is the love of the Holy Trinity for all of us. If our LORD JESUS became man to ransom us and save us, the least we could do, and for sure our LORD would be pleased, is to offer everything to Him. Whenever and whatever we offer to GOD, we should always do it in JESUS' name. Offering everything entails not only the Sacramental services, not only our community services, but even our nothingness. Always give your thanks for everything, too. Extend your gratitude and always say it in JESUS' name.

Another powerful tool in casting out evil spirits is by praying this, "In the Name of JESUS, I cast you out demon!" Remember, our LORD JESUS is the Name above all names. So when you pray, always end your prayer with, (We pray this In the Name of JESUS, Amen!)

> LORD GOD, I thank You for everything. I know for a fact that every time I pray, "In JESUS name", I really feel good and I feel the deep love and mercy of JESUS' redemption. And all of this is, because of Your graces. I pray for all the graces that I need LORD in my every actions, in JESUS' name I pray, Amen!
> 08/19/01

Esther B. Jimenez

PRAISE THE ALMIGHTY

Daniel 3 : 57

Bless the LORD, all you works of the LORD, praise and exalt Him above all forever.

When was the last time you praised GOD and exalted His name? The great thing I learned from joining a charismatic group is, singing, clapping, raising hands, even dancing, swinging your body, closing your eyes, and proclaiming GOD's greatness, kindness and goodness, vocally. Praying vocally and singing loud, shouting for joy, doubles the prayer. Every form of prayer is good enough for GOD. He is an understanding GOD. All He cares about is our welfare; our souls and our relationship with His Son. He knows what our needs are, but He loves to hear you say you love Him. Why don't you start praising Him everyday, worshipping and honoring Him? Tell our LORD how much you are grateful and always exalt His glorious name. Let us praise the Almighty!

If you want to know how you could start praising GOD, start by opening your Bible to the Psalms of David. There are 150 chapters in the Book of Psalms and most of the verses are praising, worshipping and honoring our Creator. Again, praise GOD all the time, praise the Almighty! Alleluia!

> LORD GOD, I praise You, I worship You and I honor You with profound reverence. I glorify and magnify Your name. You are an awesome GOD. You are my Great Healer, my Confidant, my Savior, my Fortress, my Advocate and my Everything! I love You and I bless You! I pray this in JESUS' name Amen!
> 08/19/01

Bible Tidbits

BE PREPARED

Matthew 25 : 13

Therefore, stay awake, for you know neither the day nor the hour.

I was not a girl scout, but I remember I had a playmate when I was in school, who was a boy scout. That was the first time I learned about the famous motto, "Be Prepared". Two simple words, but very authoritative, powerful words.

We do a lot of preparation in our lives, such as: preparing the kids at school's opening, we have wedding preparations, we prepare for the coming baby, even for speakers (they prepare for their speech) and not to forget there are Christmas preparations and many more to mention. Being prepared is being ready and being orderly,(putting our lives in order).

What we failed to realize and failed to recognize is, the need of preparation of the second coming of our LORD JESUS CHRIST. This is the most important and crucial preparation of all. Why don't we start preparing for our LORD JESUS' second coming no matter how busy we are? All you have to do is to ask GOD's grace. He will help you prepare. Just tell Him, you are offering your concerns to Him. Of course, you must also be ready for His help. He will know what's in your heart. So let us be all boys scouts and girls scouts and follow the motto, "Be Prepared".

> LORD GOD, it is indeed true that we don't know when Your Son is coming. No one knows one's future. But I thank You for showing me the way to prepare for His coming, in JESUS' name I pray, Amen!
> 08/19/03

Esther B. Jimenez

SIMPLE REQUEST

1 John 3 : 23

And His commandment is this; we should believe in the name of His Son, JESUS CHRIST, and love one another just as he commanded us.

All of us are blessed and gifted, Christians or non-Christians, because of the fact that JESUS CHRIST suffered for us. We are blessed because of the faith we have and we are gifted because we have the gifts of belief that JESUS CHRIST is LORD.

Atheists and agnostics don't believe in GOD, they don't have the view of who JESUS is? Some people don't want to believe in JESUS' existence, but they believe in their higher power. Nothing is wrong with that, at least they believe in something.

Our LORD has a simple request, that is to believe in JESUS and to love one another. I know it is not difficult to love one another, Christians or non-Christians. It is up to us then if you want to follow the entire requests, (GOD'S precepts and commandments.) GOD will lead us to the right direction, but He will give us the freedom to choose.

LORD GOD, thank you for Your commandments, and thank You I was born Catholic Christian. Grant me the grace to love the people who hurt me. May You continue to allow me to imitate JESUS and may I see JESUS in everyone's face. Most of all thank You for the gift of faith and belief that JESUS CHRIST is LORD. I pray all this in JESUS' name Amen!
08/19/01

Bible Tidbits

LAST WORDS

Acts 7 : 59

As they were stoning Stephen, he called out, "LORD JESUS, receive my spirit".

What will be your last words, when you'll be in a near death situation?

One time, me and my friends talked about near-death last wishes and last words. We asked each other on what would be our last words, before we die. And here are some of their answers: One says, "I will say the Our Father", the other one says, "Hail Mary and Glory Be", and the last one says, "Amen". I told them that I will ask GOD's forgiveness right away, "Forgive me LORD, for my sins." Then I'll do the sign of the cross.

You see, we don't even know if the words mentioned above would be the actual words that would be said, in an actual situation.

I had a car accident four years ago, and I thought that was the end of my life.

My first impulse was to grab the rosary hanging on the rear view mirror. And as soon as I reached the emergency room, I requested a priest and when the priest came he gave me communion (Eucharistic Host). It's indeed GOD's miracle, that I survived. I really encourage you to ask GOD from now on, the grace of peaceful preparation for your last moments. Stephen asked JESUS to receive His spirit. This is a very humble and noble request. We can be Stephen, too can't we?

> LORD GOD, I pray that I may receive your forgiveness and blessings before I die. I pray also for all the souls in purgatory and for all the dying spirits. St. Stephen, be with us in time of our death, with JESUS at your side, in JESUS' name, I pray, Amen!
> 08/19/01

Esther B. Jimenez

FOOTPRINTS

Isaiah 30 : 19

O people of Zion, who dwell in Jerusalem no more will you weep; He will be gracious to you, when you cry out, as soon as he hears he will answer you.

GOD answers prayers. If prayers are not answered at the time you needed them, most probably there are valid reasons. And if you would ask GOD's grace, and ask the Holy Spirit for the gift of wisdom, He will let you know why the prayers were not answered.

We often hear the phrase, "In His Time", yes your prayers will be answered in His Time. It is very true that GOD answers in His time and in His own mysterious ways. GOD doesn't give things you can't handle and he doesn't give problems. He gives solutions to the problems. He will help you carry those problems, as He said in the poem, "Footprints In The Sand". He said, "I never left you during your times of trial and suffering. When you see only one set of footprints, it was then, that, I was carrying you". So, trust in the LORD in good times and bad times, too.

LORD GOD, You are greater than my problems, greater than all of our problems. I thank You for the gift of calmness, that I no longer panic or become anxious about any of my problems. I leave everything in Your care. Thank You for You never left me. I will always follow You and look at the footprints that symbolize Your Presence, LORD, I pray all this in JESUS' name, Amen!
08/19/01

Bible Tidbits

THE RESCUER

Luke 21 : 36

"Be vigilant at all times and pray that you have the strength to escape the tribulations that are imminent and to stand before the Son of Man."

There is an adage that says, "When it rains it pours". Imagine having one problem after another problem. Motivational speakers will tell you to be a positive thinker and to face your problems. And the Scriptures say, "Be vigilant at all times and pray that you have the strength…" Be always on the lookout, be watchful and be prepared. Like I said in the previous pages, GOD is greater than any problems. Just pray and ask Him to guide you every step of the way. The strength that He'll give is the weapon to use to overcome your tribulations. Also, remember that our LORD is always ready to rescue us from any tribulations. He will not abandon us. He will answer our prayers, and He will give us spiritual strength. So don't call 911, instead call 1-800 – PRAYERS, and THE RESCUER will be there. Actually, He is already there, before you even call Him. Here is how to call Him:

P- raise GOD! The
R- escuer!
A- cclaim His Goodness
Y- ield to the Holy Spirit
E- xalt His Name! For He
R- edeems and
S- aves us!

LORD GOD, I ask You to grant me the strength to face all my trials. Transform my trials and tribulations into triumphs. I thank You for helping me all the time and for not abandoning me, in JESUS' name I pray, Amen!
08/19/01

Esther B. Jimenez

INSEPARABLE

Romans 8 : 38 –39

38 For I am convinced that neither death, nor life, nor angels, nor principalities, nor present things, nor future things, nor powers 39 nor height, nor depth, nor any other creature will be able to separate us from the love of GOD in CHRIST JESUS our LORD.

This is one of my favorite verses in the Bible. I could feel the power of GOD's love. This is the strongest bonding among all relationships in this world. How can we not see it? How can we not know this?

This is something that we can really be proud of, reassuring ourselves that no one can just separate us from GOD's love, in CHRIST JESUS. This will erase all the doubts in our hearts, because peace will be in our hearts forever.

I am not saying this because it is written in the Bible. I indeed use this as my weapon in my trials and tribulations and also in my personal encounters with unpleasant people. But again, we have to ask the grace from GOD to put His Word in our hearts, so we can use His Word divinely.

> LORD GOD, I thank You for the reassurance, for Your faithfulness and for Your Word. Grant me LORD the grace to continue pondering and reflecting on these verses, so that I can use them in my daily encounters and in every moment of temptation. I ask You to forgive me LORD all the time. I know that even sins can't separate us, for You are a forgiving GOD and You'll give us the gift of repentance. Thank You for the reassurance that You and mankind are inseparable. All this I pray in JESUS' name Amen!
> 08/19/01

MIND OUR OWN BUSINESS

Luke 6 : 41

Why do you notice the splinter in your brother's eye, but do not perceive the wooden beam in your own?

Criticisms can be constructive and destructive. I always believe that whatever you do or say, depends on the intention of the heart. If you want to correct or criticize someone and your intention is to embarrass that person, that is unruly and humiliating. But if your intention is for improvement and betterment of that person, that is caring and compassion.

Before you say something unpleasant to someone, look at the mirror and look at yourself and do a little bit of self-analysis. You might find out that you are doing the same thing or you might be worse than that person. Or better yet, that person might be your model for your own transformation. We can't just judge people.

So why don't we mind our own business? Let us stop counting our neighbor's faults. The next time you want to correct someone, do it in a Christian way; don't be judgmental. Remember to check your own splinter, before checking others.

> LORD GOD, I thank You for removing the splinter in my eye. I see things now in a Christian way, because of the grace You have given me. I pray LORD that You would guide my thoughts, guard my actions and tame my tongue. I ask this and pray in JESUS' name Amen!
> 08/20/01

Esther B. Jimenez

THE BEST CHOICE

Joshua 24 : 15

If it does not please you to serve the LORD, decide today whom you will serve, the gods your fathers served beyond the River or the gods of the Amorites in whose country you are dwelling. As for me and my household, we will serve the LORD.

Have you been in a situation, that you were given two choices? To serve or not to serve?

I thank GOD that every member in our family is serving the LORD, through a Catholic community service. I thank GOD for He allows me to be a Eucharistic Minister in my parish church. Whatever you do in life, the Best Choice is to serve Him and ask Him the way He wants to be served. He will lead you, because He knows best. GOD doesn't force people; He gives us freedom to choose. And if you ask Him for the grace to do His will, He will grant it to you. Don't forget to ask the Holy Spirit too, to give you the gift of discernment.

With the Holy Trinity around us all the time, we'll be guided of the Best Choice.

LORD GOD, I thank You for calling us to serve You, the way You wanted to be served. Thank You for touching our lives and thank You for all the blessings. We bless You and we love You LORD. I pray this in JESUS' name Amen!
08/20/01

Bible Tidbits

CONSTRUCTIVE CRITICISM

Matthew 18 : 15

"If your brother sins (against you), go and tell him his fault between you and him alone. If he listens to you, you have won over your brother.

Confrontation is the best approach for correcting someone; or telling someone about the hurt that he has caused. In simple terms, it is called, "1:1 session". The advantage of a confrontation is, it will be more effective, because the topic of the conversation is more focused. Confronting someone is also very professional especially in the business level or at the workplace. Even the children in the family, if you embarrass them in front of anybody, especially in front of their friends, will retaliate or they will lose their respect for you. So constructive criticism is really appropriate and will produce better results.

Confrontation is not only productive, but it is a proper channel of communication. So when you get the chance to correct someone, use this Christian approach.

LORD GOD, thank You for giving me the gift of diplomacy, that I always approach people in a diplomatic way. Please guide me in dealing with difficult people, and give me LORD, the gift of understanding and most of all the grace of humility. I pray this in JESUS' name Amen!
08/20/01

Esther B. Jimenez

ANIMALS AND PETS

Matthew 10 : 16

"Behold, I am sending you like sheep in the midst of wolves; so be shrewd as serpents and simple as doves".

Animals and pets have different characteristics and behaviors. The Chinese have different animal symbols and each animal portrays different signs. Every year there is a certain animal that they consider the "birth year" as, "year of the dragon", "year of the pig"," year of the rat", etc.

I like animals and pets. They are GOD's creations too. Sometimes we are being compared to a certain animal or pet, because of our attitude, behavior, manner, strength, weakness, and other things.

Actually our instincts are responsible for our behavior. And that is the difference between animals/pets and mankind. We can be like animals, if we act as one. We can admire their good qualities and acquire them as well.

If you are to choose what animal or pet would you be, what would you choose? Me? I want to be simple like the doves, calm as the lambs, faithful as the dogs, sweet as the birds, strong as the lions, and to think big like the elephants.(Actually, elephants don't think big) but because they are huge, it represent a big scope.

Again we can learn more from animals and pets, so be kind to them.

LORD GOD, thank You for all Your creatures. I thank You for my own pets, which I consider as my best friends. I pray that people would be kind to animals and pets. Those who are cruel to animals and pets and insects, bless them and change their hearts to kindness. Bless all of us, LORD, Your creations and creatures in JESUS' name I pray Amen!
08/20/01

BE ASSERTIVE…IN A CHRISTIAN WAY

Matthew 5 : 39

But I say to you, offer no resistance to one who is evil. When someone strikes you on (your) right cheek, turn the other one to him as well.

If you turn your other cheek, after the one has been hurt, it is the same as, "throwing a bread when someone throws you a stone".

Indeed, it is tempting to get even or to get back, at the people that hurt us or do us evil. In my life I had a lot of chances to get revenge on the people who have hurt me, or who were mean to me, but GOD was so good to me. He was always intercepting my vengeful plans. I am glad that in this stage of my life, my transformed life, I am able to handle my hurt and humiliation in a Christian way. Yes, I still assert myself, but in a divine way now, not getting upset. And gee! It is a great feeling and great accomplishment, to deal with such things in a Christian way.

LORD GOD, thank You for the gift of understanding, the gift of humility, the gift of self-control, the gift of diplomacy and most of all the gift of Christian assertiveness. May You continue to grant me the graces that I need, in my daily encounters. I pray all this in JESUS' name Amen!
08/20/01

Esther B. Jimenez

HOLY REPLACEMENT

Ephesians 4 : 31 –32

31…All bitterness, fury, anger, shouting, and reviling must be removed from you, along with all malice, 32…(And) be kind to one another, compassionate, forgiving one another as GOD has forgiven you in CHRIST.

What we are today, is rooted in how we were brought up. Our past experiences have something to do with what we are today. Our bitterness, our anger, our rebellious actions and other negative attitudes were rooted from what we call, "life psycho-dynamics", the upbringing process.

Let's forget the psycho-dynamic thing. Let's stop blaming our past. Let's look forward for the chance to change. If we can be kind to one another and be compassionate, and be forgiving, we will be better persons. And we can make the difference in this world. Again we can only accomplish these through GOD's grace. So let us start working on our Holy Replacement. Let us replace our negative attitudes with positive attitudes; our anger with compassion; our pride with humility; and our unforgiving hearts with forgiveness. Let us look forward for more Holy Replacements. I guarantee you we'll never run out of these replacements. They are there, ready for us.

> LORD GOD, You are a forgiving GOD. I thank You for forgiving me all the time. Please continue to grant me many Holy Replacements and the grace to perform Christian deeds, I pray this in JESUS' name Amen!
> 08/20/01

LENGTHEN THE LENT SEASON

Tobit 12 : 8

Prayer and fasting are good, but better than either is almsgiving accompanied by righteousness. A little with righteousness is better than abundance with wickedness. It is better to give alms than to store up gold.

Prayer, fasting and almsgiving are the three important things to do during Lent season. Lent or not Lent we should pray, fast and give alms. These three are the keys to the answering of prayers. These are essential in asking graces from GOD.
So let us lengthen our Lent season.
When we pray, we should pray from our hearts and we must do it fervently. When we fast, we should be sincere and be meditative. When we give alms, let's be more generous and be faithful stewards.
Whatever you do, be righteous; that is the bottom line. Let us rejoice, for our GOD is in our hearts. Let us lengthen Lent, for GOD loves a person with a prayerful, humble and generous heart.

LORD GOD, I am overwhelmed with Your greatness, kindness and goodness. I am always inspired to write about You. I love to share my experiences with You, and with my sisters and brothers in CHRIST. I thank You for everything my LORD, in JESUS' name I pray, Amen!
08/20/01

Esther B. Jimenez

GENUINE FRIENDSHIP

Sirach 6 : 5 – 6

5 A kind mouth multiplies friends, and gracious lips prompt friendly greetings. 6 Let your acquaintances be many, but one in a thousand your confidant.

How do you choose a friend? How do you keep a friend? How do you know if that person is a true and genuine friend?

I have learned a lot about this friendship business. I can't just reveal my true self until I know that I could trust a person. That's what I think. But on three occasions, I have been betrayed by friends. I am now very careful, and I always pray for every dealing I make with people I meet. I know I can be friendly, actually I am very friendly, that's why I am vulnerable to being hurt. But I know now the difference between friendly and being trustful. At present time, I have at least two genuine friends that I could really trust. I prayed for these two friends and I treasured their friendship, especially they are my friends in CHRIST. Do you have a true and genuine friend? If you do, keep him. If you don't have, ask GOD to give you true and genuine one. If you want to read more about friendship, please read:

Sirach 9 : 10-16.

LORD GOD, I am blessed with true and genuine friends. I thank You for giving me such friends. Grant me LORD the grace of faithfulness, to be faithful to You and to them. You are my Best Friend and my true and genuine Friend. I trust my friends, but I trust You with my life. I pray for every genuine friendship, in JESUS' name Amen!

08/20/01

PERSONAL APPEARANCE

1 John 4; 12

No one has ever seen GOD. Yet, if we love one another, GOD remains in us, and his love is brought to perfection in us.

In the Old Testament, Abraham, Moses and some prophets have seen the LORD. There is a word that describes this face to face meeting with GOD. It is called, "theopany". Theopany is a direct communication with GOD and an appearance of GOD to human beings. The Incarnation of GOD proves to us that a lot of people in the New Testament really have seen the LORD'S face, through CHRIST JESUS. We should not be jealous, because we will be given the same opportunity, in His time. The love we have for one another, and our being Christian in the true sense, is our proof that we see GOD in our hearts.

As I've mentioned on the previous pages, we can see JESUS in everyone's face. Let us just wait for the time of His personal appearance.

> LORD GOD, what a great opportunity it is, to see Your Son in everyone's face. I thank You for letting me know about the "theopany" in the Old Testament. I pray for that right time to see You and embrace You LORD. Grant me the gift of wisdom to know the truth behind "theopany". I will continue my LORD to serve You and to love You. I pray all this in JESUS' name Amen!
> 08/20/01

Esther B. Jimenez

DEGREE OF LOVE

John 15 : 13

No one has greater love than this, to lay down one's life for one's friends.

I wrote down something about true friendship on the previous pages. Sirach gives a good description of friendship and tips on how to choose a friend. I think laying down your life for a friend is a very noble gesture, a heroic action, I may say. It is a sincere intention. The degree of love is detected from the depth of the love you give. And that's the kind of love our LORD JESUS is giving us. In return He expects us to follow His Footsteps. Maximillian Kolbe offered his life just to free a prisoner. Soldiers lay down their lives for their countries.

Offering service to fellowmen, help at church, the hospital, the community, or being missionaries, are signs of love.

Our GOD is pleased with simple acts like these. The degree of love is measured from the heart. Love is powerful. This has been proven many, many times by our LORD JESUS.

Shall I remind you about His sufferings, to redeem our sins? No one can beat that kind of love.

LORD GOD, You sent Your Son, to ransom us and to show Your love for us. Your love is enough for me. Your love is my treasure and wealth. Grant me LORD the spirit of dedication. I pray this in JESUS' name Amen!
08/21/01

Bibi Tidbits

RENEWED LIFE

1 Peter 5 : 10

The GOD of all grace who called you to His eternal glory through CHRIST (JESUS), will himself restore, confirm, strengthen, and establish you after you have suffered a little.

Our LORD JESUS' sufferings are greater than our sufferings. Do you know the feeling of being transformed? Have you felt the process of transformation? If you do, you know that whatever you do or say, you'll be guided by the Holy Spirit, if you ask for it. The way I handle my problems now is different, than the way I handled my problems before. I don't focus on my problems anymore, because I have strong faith that GOD is always there to help me. GOD is greater than my problems. He is giving me spiritual strength for my problems.

He is giving me spiritual growth and leading me to the spiritual pathway. Not only that, He is granting me spiritual connection with my loved ones. My conversion and transformation is through GOD's grace. My renewed life brings peace to my heart.

LORD GOD, thank You for suffering for us; for giving us spiritual strength; for the spiritual direction; and spiritual connection with my loved ones. I ask LORD that You may grant me more graces and mercy as I go on with my life. Thank You for my renewal. In JESUS' name I pray, Amen!
08/21/01

Esther B. Jimenez

BEYOND CONTROL

Psalm 46 : 2 – 3

2 GOD is our refuge and our strength, an ever present help in distress. 3 Thus we do not fear, though earth be shaken and mountains quake to the depths of the sea.

Calamities and disasters are part of nature, and when they occur, it is beyond our control. We are scared of lightning, thunderstorms, earthquakes, deluges, hurricanes, tornadoes and heavy floods. But they are all belong to nature. Again, GOD is greater than any calamities and disasters. We have to remember that He is our Refuge and He will give us the strength that we need, to cope with any of those calamities and disasters.

Be prepared, that is another thing we can do. But the most important thing is to always "pray", with or without calamities. It is only our Creator who has the control. Everything is beyond our control.

LORD GOD, You are indeed our Refuge and our Strength. You are my Consolation and my Hope. I thank You for being with me during my personal stormy weather. I ask that You will hold my hands and will lead me to the right pathway. I pray this in JESUS' name Amen!
08/21/01

PATHWAY OF THE JUST

Hosea 14 : 10

Let him who is wise understand these things; let him who is prudent know them. Straight are the paths of the LORD, in them the just walk; but sinners stumble in them.

No one in this world has ever been just and prudent without GOD's grace. We can't be just and prudent through our own will. GOD has to be in the middle of that will, because it will be His will that will transform us. Our willingness is the key and our repentance is a start. Blessed are those who are willing to transform their lives. The realization and the wisdom that the "just" possessed, indeed came from GOD. The transformation starts from GOD's call, then, your willingness, and then your acceptance of His Son. So, if GOD starts calling you, don't hesitate to say yes. Remember, you have tried many times, the sinners way, why not try the just way this time? You'll know if GOD is calling you, so wait for His call.

Just ask Him to give you the grace of openness and willingness. The pathway of the just starts from a rough road, until you reach the straight-smooth road.

LORD GOD, I thank You for calling me and for the gift of obedience. Thank You for saving me from the bumpy road, where I was before. Grant me LORD, the grace of discipline to avoid the crooked road. Help me not to stumble again. I pray this in JESUS' name Amen!
08/22/01

Esther B. Jimenez

THE REAL QUENCHER

Psalm 42 : 3

My being thirsts for GOD, the living GOD. When can I go and see the face of GOD?

Have you ever experienced extreme thirst? Then you tried to pacify yourself by drinking cold drinks, soda or juice? Then you are still thirsty and finally the last result, water? Well, that is the physical aspect of thirst. That is not the real quencher. Experiencing thirst is experiencing emptiness in ones life. No matter what you do to make yourself happy or content or even to have peace, you can never be satisfied.

Why? Because we are craving for the Real Quencher. It's only GOD, Who can fill our emptiness, (the emptiness of extreme thirst).

The next time you feel empty, ponder on GOD's greatness and gauge yourself, find out how your relationship with Him is. Wherever you go, you will never feel thirsty if you have Him in your heart, the Real Quencher.

LORD GOD, I know that You thirst for us, too…for our repentance and our transformation. I thirst for Your love and mercy. Thank You for being our Real Quencher. I pray this in JESUS' name Amen!
08/22/01

Bible Tidbits

THE BEST INVITATION

Jeremiah 50 : 5

….Come, let us join ourselves to the LORD with the covenant everlasting, never to be forgotten.

    Do you always attend parties or gatherings, every time you're invited? How about joining social groups, attending seminars, campaigning, have you accepted those kind of invitations?

    There is always a reason for accepting invitation. It could be that you enjoy the company of a friend; or you want to learn something if it is a seminar, or you want to support a candidate if it is a political campaign; or you just want to loosen up from a tiring job, and many more reasons.

    The word, "Come" is a very powerful word in the Bible. It has been mentioned many times, because our LORD JESUS CHRIST always uses this, in inviting people, whether to heal them or to preach to them or to teach them. Joining GOD's assembly is the Best Invitation. If anyone invites you for a retreat, or teachings from your parish church, Bible study or Christian gatherings, give it a thought. It may be a call from GOD. GOD's invitation is the Best Invitation.

    LORD GOD, thank You for inviting me to join You in attending every congregation. Thank You for the retreats that I have attended especially with the speaker priests. Thank You for all the homilies in all the Masses. Most of all thank You for Your call, the Best Invitation. I pray this in JESUS' name Amen!
08/22/01

HUMILITY

Matthew 23 : 12

Whoever exalts himself will be humbled; but whoever humbles himself will be exalted.

Humility is one of the greatest virtues. I never realized that humility takes a lot of giving up; (1) pride, (2) vanity, (3) obsession, (4) possession, and (5) materialism.

Now, are you ready to give up all those things mentioned or may be one at a time?

Another important thing in relation to humility, is forgiveness. I think it is the hardest thing to do. But it is possible with GOD's grace and also with the help of the Holy Spirit. Be open to the gift of humility.

Let me share with you what's behind the gift of humility. First, you'll find joy, second, you'll have contentment and third, you'll have peace in your heart.

The three virtues can be experienced only when you learn to forgive, when you learn to acknowledge your own mistakes and when you learn to ask for forgiveness.

And the secret of attaining peace is, "always choose to have less rather than more", (this is from the book entitled, "The Imitation of CHRIST" by Thomas A. Kempis)

Lastly, humility is the acknowledgement of the truth and the absolute foundation of spiritual life.

LORD GOD, I am thankful and grateful for I learned to be humble. Thank You for the gift of humility. LORD, make me more humble today than yesterday, make me more humble tomorrow than today, all this I pray in JESUS' name Amen!
08/23/01

DESIRE TO SERVE

1 Peter 5 : 2

Tend the flock of GOD in your midst, (overseeing) not by constraint but willingly, as GOD would have it, not for shameful profit but eagerly.

Everyone of us belongs to the flock of GOD. But there are people divinely delegated as flock care-givers. If you are one of them, remember, GOD wants you to have a desire to serve. Do you serve with love and compassion?

Maybe you are a leader of a certain group; maybe you're a doctor, or a nurse, or a police officer, or anyone who gives service to people. The thing that I am trying to point out is, the desirability of a person to serve. There should be willingness and concern in rendering service of any sort. Service with love and compassion makes our LORD happy, because He knows you are tending His flock and treating them right.

Remember when JESUS asked Peter three times if he loves Him and Peter answered, "Yes" three times, too? And JESUS said, "Feed my lambs" and "Tend my sheep", and, "Feed my sheep", respectively. Peter loved JESUS so much and he had a strong desire to serve Him. Do we have that kind of desire? I dare you to desire!

LORD GOD, as I'm writing this book, the more I feel You are inside me, letting me feel the desire to serve You. I can't thank You enough for the messages and the wisdom that You have given me. Thank You for the gift of willingness and the desire to serve. Grant me LORD, Your constant blessings. I love You and I bless You, in JESUS' name I pray, Amen!
08/23/01

Esther B. Jimenez

Let me share a stanza from my poem, "A Desire To Serve"

Willingness, spoken from the heart,
Servant hood, the way it must,
A call to serve a desire I have
Ministry of service, let me accept.
Please lead me where it demands,
Thank You LORD for the chance,
To offer my moments of life,
To work on Your plans, feeding Your lambs.

COURAGEOUS WOMAN

Esther C : 23

Be mindful of us, O LORD. Manifest yourself in the time of our distress and give me courage, King of gods and Ruler of every power.

Courage is a positive attitude and another great virtue. It seems it's a masculine word. Is courage for men only? I don't think so. There are a few courageous women in the Bible and Esther is one of them. She is not only courageous, but she is beautiful too. She is a prayerful woman. She prays for every decision and every plan she makes. That's why she was successful in her plot. What plot? Please read the Bible if you could. She really asked the LORD to give her the grace of courage. And she received it. She praises GOD all the time and acclaims Him as the Ruler of every power. I really am encouraging you to read the chapter about Esther. Let us follow her Christian ways and her courageousness.

LORD GOD, thank You for creating us in Your Image. Thank You for the grace that You have given me. I need to be more courageous LORD, to surpass the obstacles in my life. Thank You for the women in the Bible who inspired me. May You bless all the women in this world. I pray this in JESUS' name Amen!
08/23/01

Esther B. Jimenez

GOD'S DIVINE STRATEGY

Ezekiel 18 : 23

Do I indeed derive any pleasure from the death of the wicked? says the LORD GOD. Do I not rather rejoice when he turns from his evil way that he may live?

GOD is not interested with the morbidity rate nor mortality rate. He is interested with our performance rate. GOD knows we are sinners. He knows we are stubborn. He knows our vices, our vanities, our life styles, our thoughts and our hearts. Most of all He knows our weaknesses.

It is intriguing to know that when He created us, He started His divine strategy with the original couple. Then something happened that proved the couple's weakness. And you know the rest of the story, the story of the creation. GOD didn't stop there. He still use His divine strategy with the prophets. Same thing happened, more sinners, more sinning.

Now, the best divine strategy came. Finally, our LORD thought of revising His strategy. He then sent His Son to start redeeming sins, gathering them and offering His sufferings for our salvation.

Before the moments of our LORD JESUS CHRIST'S passion, He did a lot of miracles, healing, preaching and teaching through His well known parables. A lot of moral lessons were gained by the disciples and other followers. GOD's Divine Strategy is from Creation to Revelation.

LORD GOD, thank You for giving me a chance to transform my life. Thank You for allowing me to know You more and to know Your Son JESUS. Thank You for the Divine Strategy. I pray LORD that You will continue to forgive us and may You help us every step of the way, in JESUS' name Amen!
08/23/01

FEED THE NEEDY

Isaiah 58 : 7

Sharing your bread with the hungry, sheltering the oppressed and the homeless; Clothing the naked when you see them, and not turning your back on your own.

The Beatitudes tell us so much about how blessed are the poor and the needy and the oppressed.

If you are feeding the poor, clothing the naked, visiting the prisoner, it is our LORD that you are feeding, clothing and visiting, respectively. As the Scriptures say, "If you do all these to your brothers, you do them unto Him".

There is a well known non-profit organization name, "RAK" (Random Act of Kindness). It is located almost all over the States and other countries. They have lists of ideas on how you can show your kindness to everyone, to every group, randomly or planned.

Every year we celebrate Thanksgiving Day, and a lot of non-profit organizations again sponsor food drives, meals, rooming-in homeless people, especially in some churches. Some families and some individuals volunteer to serve and some prepare their own soup and sandwiches for a certain number of people.

How about us? How about you? How can we contribute?

Have you seen on the television about the "less than a dollar a day" donation for the needy? Would you want to consider that?

There are seven corporal works of mercy; to feed the hungry; to give drink to the thirsty; to clothe the naked; to visit the imprisoned; to shelter the homeless; to visit the sick and to bury the dead. Just ponder on these, will you?

LORD GOD, I am lucky because I can still have at least three meals a day. I really bless the poor, the homeless, with my fervent prayers. I thank You for Your kindness, love and mercy. I pray this in JESUS' name Amen!
08/23/01

Esther B. Jimenez

REMEMBER!!! TO FORGET

Hebrews 8 : 12

For I will forgive their evil doing and remember their sins no more.

"To err is human, to forgive is divine" as the saying goes. Forgiveness is one of the most popular topics or issues, being discussed in the prayer groups and even favorite gossip topics.

It's one of the causes of family feuds, i.e. having an unforgiving family member.

Forgiving is one of the solutions for family reconciliation.

I used to be scared and felt uneasy every time I heard the word, "forgive". Maybe because of my high pride. And I always used to stick with my principle that, "if it wasn't my fault I won't make the first move"; meaning no apology, no asking of forgiveness nor forgiveness on my part. But now, that is my favorite word. I can talk about it, preach about it and practice it as well. On the previous page, I touched about the number of times a person must forgive.

And I mentioned that forgiving but not forgetting is as good as not forgiving at all. Remember!!! To forget and forgive. Maybe this one will be better, "forgetting first then forgive".

I would like to share a stanza from one of my poems entitled, "Embrace Your Hurt, Embrace JESUS".

> **When you're hurt and can't forgive,**
> **It is even hard to imitate JESUS,**
> **For He says, we need to do it seventy-seven times,**
> **LORD JESUS, we need the grace to**
> **forgive and be forgiven.**

LORD GOD, I thank You for the gift of humility and the grace of reconciliation. Forgive me LORD for all my wrong doings. Thank You for Your love and mercy. Continue LORD to transform my life. I pray all this in JESUS' name, Amen!
08/23/01

RESPECT

1 Corinthians 6 : 19

Do you not know that your body is a temple of the Holy Spirit within you, whom you have from GOD, and that you are not your own?

Whoever you are now, is what GOD has given you. Whatever you do with what GOD has given you, is your gift to GOD. Remember how GOD created the first couple, it was almost perfect until the original sin caused its imperfection.

One essence of the Ten Commandments is respect for oneself and respect for others. Whatever sin you committed your body is affected. So do not tamper your body either physically or spiritually. Respect your body because it is the temple of the Holy Spirit.

Bear in mind that we are created in GOD's Image. We should respect our own bodies and be aware of how we handle ourselves, the way we dress, the way we move and most of all how we value our values. If we respect our bodies, we are respectful of the Holy Spirit, too.

LORD GOD, thank You for creating me in Your Image. Grant me the gift of awareness, in taking care of my body, be physically or spiritually. Thank You for the gift of respect, in JESUS' name I pray Amen!
08/23/01

Esther B. Jimenez

EXPERIENCE IS THE BEST TEACHER

Hebrews 2 : 18

Because he himself was tested through what he suffered, he is able to help those who are being tested.

Skill is a term used for a person with a lot of experience. Everyone of us must be good at something. That's what an expert is. You can be effective in whatever skills you have, or you can be expert if you use those skills to help somebody out.

Our LORD GOD sent His Son and became man. He suffered and died for us. And during JESUS' suffering He tried to bear every wound and every ridicule that He received. But He is not regretful. He even teaches us to bear our own wounds, to sanctify ourselves, to mortify our lives for a good cause.

He shows us a lot of virtues to use. Our LORD JESUS CHRIST is the Best Teacher forever. He shares all His experiences with all mankind.

LORD GOD, I thank You and I praise You. I honor You with profound reverence. I respect You for being my Best Teacher. I bless the wounds that You received. Thank You for the virtues that You have given me, in JESUS' name, I pray, Amen!
08/24/01

Bible Tidbits

YOUR CHANCE AND MINE

Mark 1 : 15

This is the time of fulfillment. The Kingdom of GOD is at hand. Repent and believe in the gospel.

Two striking words, "Repent and Believe", and for some of us, we really don't care about these words. But for some these are words of reminder, words of advice and most of all they are words from the Holy Book.

There are four "R's" that I thought should be considered, in the process of repentance. (1) Realization of the existence of evil whispers that push us to commit sins;(2) Reconsideration of acknowledging our sins (make amends); (3) Reconciliation with the persons concerned, (asking forgiveness), and be forgiving at the same time; (4) Recording the process in your mind and put it in your heart and start believing that all these are the powerful words of our LORD JESUS CHRIST in the Bible. Make the process of repentance a part of your daily encounters.

Now that we are given the same chances, what are we going to do with those chances? Let us grab them! Remember, the Kingdom of GOD is at hand. This is your chance and mine.

LORD GOD, thank You for Your Holy reminder about repentance. Thank You for the wisdom that You just gave me, about the four R's (the process of repentance). Grant us LORD the graces that we need in our transformation and repentance. Thank You for Your love and mercy. I pray this in JESUS' name, Amen!
08/24/01

Esther B. Jimenez

COME O HOLY SPIRIT, COME

Romans 8 : 26

In the same way, the Spirit too comes to the aid of our weakness; for we do not know how to pray as we ought, but the Spirit itself interferes with inexpressible groanings.

Prayer is a powerful word. It is mentioned in the Bible many, many times.

There are thousands of Christian books written about prayer. In the Old Testament, there were a lot of prayers mentioned. Some prophets prayed through their offerings, some through fasting, some through songs and psalms as in the Book of Psalms (David's Psalms).

In the New Testament, JESUS taught His disciples how to pray the, "Our Father". There are also prayers by different Saints, novena prayers, litanies and our own individual prayers. Praying is not mere opening your mouth. The Holy Spirit aids us in our prayer moments

Have you tried asking the Holy Spirit to guide you when you pray? It is also powerful when the Holy Spirit comes to you in your prayer time, or even in random prayers. Even when you are tongue tied, the Holy Spirit will prompt you and if you will be open to His gifts, He will give you the gift of tongues, even just inexpressible groans.

Pope John Paul II mentioned in one of his writings that every time you open the Bible, you should first pray the Holy Spirit prayer. If you don't know the prayer or can't remember the prayer just say, "Come O Holy Spirit, Come".

LORD GOD, I thank You for our Constant Companion, the Holy Spirit, for His promptings, His guidance and His gifts. Grant me LORD the gift of intercession, so I can pray for other people fervently. I pray all this in JESUS name Amen!
08/24/01

GOD'S CALENDAR

Jeremiah 42 : 3

Let the LORD, your GOD, show us what way we should take and what we should do.

Picture this: A working mother wakes up in the morning, makes breakfast for two kids and a husband; prepares herself for work; goes to work; sometimes drops by the grocery after work; then prepares dinner for the family, etc. Same as business people, doctors, nurses, teachers, waiters, auto mechanics, lawyers or even plain housewives and others do. They do the same stuff everyday. Activities are routinely done. Then for some reason the routine chain breaks. Some are aggravated with the changes of the routine. Some are bored of the routines. Some become anxious, can't cope, don't know what to do, whom to call and how to solve the problems. The change of routines might be caused by tragedy, minor mishap or anything unavoidable.

What might be the possible solutions? I have one. Why don't we check GOD'S calendar. It will tell you which way to take and what should be done and how to do things. Make an appointment with Him. He is never booked up. And your name is already in His appointment book anyway. He is just waiting for you. The bottom line is, whatever you're doing, ask GOD's guidance and grace. You must be aware of His Presence. No matter what happens, you'll manage to cope and still there'll be peace in everything you do.

GOD'S calendar is our individual blueprint.

LORD GOD, I thank You for my blueprint, Your individual plan for me. I know LORD that Your calendar is always open for us. Our names are written there and I ask that You may continue to open Your calendar for all of us and may You grant us all the graces we need. I pray this in JESUS' name Amen!
08/24/01

A WIN – WIN SITUATION

1 Corinthians 15 : 49

Just as we have borne the image of the earthly one, we shall also bear the image of the heavenly one.

The movement of life is a slow process, unlike the life of the first couple, our original parents. It was an instant creation, the wonderful work of GOD.

Adam was molded from clay and the Holy Spirit blew his nostrils. Voila! A man was created. And the woman, Eve was taken from Adam's rib. What a wonderful beginning!

Each human being is a cycle of, "Womb to Tomb". Each one of us has each own destination. We are all created in GOD'S Image. And we are given the same freedom to choose. He sent His Son to redeem us. It is a win-win situation.

So love your life, it is a very precious gift. Enjoy your life to the fullest in a Christian way, and walk through GOD'S pathway.

There is another gift that is so precious awaiting us. Can you make a holy guess? It is "Eternal Life". So, no way to lose. Again, it is a win-win situation! That is the power of love, GOD'S love.

LORD GOD, thank You for the gift of life and the gift of eternal salvation. LORD, may You provide us the grace of humility and obedience, that we may realize that everything came from You. I pray this in JESUS' name Amen!
08/24/01

Bible Tidbits

LIVING WATER

John 7 : 38

Whoever believes in me, as Scripture says: Rivers of living water will flow from within Him.

Seventy five percent of our body is composed of water. The earth is surrounded by water. It seems there is no way to get thirsty. What the Scripture is saying is about spiritual drought. Our LORD JESUS is extending His invitation for us to attend His feast. Drinking juice or pop soda are not enough for our thirst. No amount of quencher will quench our thirst. This is how we will feel if we are spiritually thirsty. It is only the Living Water that can give us relief from our thirst. This figure of speech is very significant, because it tells a lot about our spiritual growth.

There is one key to this thirst, the belief that JESUS CHRIST is LORD. If you believe, without any doubt that JESUS saves us and loves us, then you can receive the flow of the Living Water, JESUS Himself.

LORD GOD, it is true that plain water can't give me relief of my thirst. I thirst for You LORD. Thank You for the Living Water that You have provided me. May You pour out Your graces and blessings, the grace of belief and understanding. Thank You for quenching us in our spiritual drought. I pray this in JESUS' name Amen!
08/25/01

THE WORD

Hebrews 4 : 12

Indeed, the word of GOD is living and effective, sharper than any two-edged sword, penetrating even between soul and spirit, joints and marrow and able to discern reflections and thoughts of the heart.

Almost everyday I hear the words, "This the word of the LORD". I go to church almost everyday, and after each reading, the lector ends with, "This is the word of the LORD".
What is the Word?
In John 1:1, it says, "In the beginning was the Word, and the Word was with GOD, and the Word was GOD". It never changed. It is in the beginning that it has already proven the power of His Word.
For me, the Word of GOD is a cure, a hope, a refuge, a promise, a miracle, a prayer, a reflection, a message, a virtue, a wisdom, a shield, and most of all a life; a life with the LORD. The Word of the LORD is always there and ready to come into our hearts. The Word of GOD is never rusty, always sharp as the two-edged sword.
GOD'S Word is never hearsay, it is always the truth. In this material world, we need very much the LORD'S Word.

LORD GOD, You are the Word. Thank You for the gift of the Word that I ponder every time I need You. Your Word is my everyday guide, so allow me to share Your Word with my loved ones, in JESUS' name I pray, Amen!
08/26/01

COME TO THE RESCUE

Psalm 59 : 2

Rescue me from my enemies, my GOD; lift me out of reach of my foes.

Imagine the work of the firemen, the EMT (Emergency Medical Technician), the doctors, the nurses, the policemen, and how they save lives. They come to the rescue.

In the Oklahoma tragedy, remember there were lots of medical teams. They treated the casualties not only physically but psychologically too. There were counselors who availed themselves during the tragedy.

I remember when I was in Saudi Arabia working as a pediatric nurse, I witnessed babies (infants) going on cardiac arrest. I experienced many times resuscitating infants. It is a great feeling when you see them revived and survived the arrest. How much more the rescue that our LORD has done all the time! He rescues us not only physically but spiritually as well. He saves our souls.

He is always there to rescue us, and He is the Team Leader of the, "Come To The Rescue" team.

LORD GOD, You are our Rescuer. You are our Savior. Thank You for Your constant guidance and protection. Help us to rebuke the abominations that surround us. Thank You for the Holy Spirit, our Constant Companion. I pray this in JESUS' name Amen!
08/29/01

Esther B. Jimenez

CO - DEPENDENCY

Psalm 23 : 1-6

1 The LORD is my shepherd; there is nothing I lack. 2 In green pastures you let me graze; to safe waters you lead me; 3 you restore my strength. You guide me along the right path for the sake of your name. 4 Even when I walk through a dark valley, I fear no harm for you are at my side; your rod and staff give me courage. 5 You set a table before me as my enemies watch; You anoint my head with oil; my cup overflows; 6 Only goodness and love will pursue me all the days of my life; I will dwell in the house of the LORD for years to come.

I never want to miss pondering on these verses. It is so popular that sometimes I wonder if they are spoken from the heart of the people reading them. Given the chance to ponder on these verses, they are indeed very powerful and you don't want to miss that chance.

The whole of Psalm 23 is talking about our dependency to GOD our Creator.

Co-dependency is a psychological illness that describes a dependency on someone or something to the extent of ruining oneself. But there is one sure dependency that is healthy, productive and effective, that is our dependency on our LORD ALMIGHTY.

Have you seen a statue or picture of JESUS holding a lamb or a sheep in His arms? And the rests of the sheep are looking at Him? That's how protective our Shepherd is. What else do we want? He is there all the time extending His love and mercy, His healing power and the chance to be with Him in His kingdom..

Two things this Psalm requests us to have, "only love and goodness", and that will pursue us all the days of our lives. Let us not only be co-dependent but let us totally be dependent on our Great Shepherd.

LORD GOD, what an inspiring message for us! The whole of Psalm 23 is already a prayer of submission and dependency on You, O LORD. I leave everything in Your care, and I pray this in JESUS' name Amen!
08/30/01

Bible Tidbits

PASS WITH FLYING COLORS

Jeremiah 17 : 10

I, the LORD, alone probe the mind and test the heart. To reward everyone according to his ways, according to the merit of his deeds.

Have you taken any examination or test lately? Were you able to make it? Did you pass with flying colors?

Passing the test of any sort has something to do with the effort to study and review.

Same thing with our relationship with our Creator. Remember the test that was given to Adam and Eve? They didn't make it. No flying colors and darkness started instead.

Our LORD knows us. He knows our minds and hearts. He even knows if we are cheating or not.

Aiming and attaining flying colors from GOD is difficult and different. And of course the reward is different too. Difficult, but challenging.

Imagine if you pass with flying colors, it will be a great feeling, because you'll have the real wisdom, not only intellectually, but spiritually. You'll have a lot of gifts, graces and virtues and you'll learn to apply them in your daily life journey. All you have to do is to say, "Yes", and be ready for the test. He will guide you every step of the way. Your transformation is a big step. So are you ready to pass with flying colors?

LORD GOD, You are an awesome GOD, allowing me to be transformed. Thank You for calling me and guiding me in every tests that You have given me. I would be facing more tests so please continue to help me pass with flying colors each time. I pray this in JESUS' name Amen!
09/01/01

NO EXCEPTION

1 Thessalonians 5 : 18

In all circumstances give thanks, for this is the will of GOD for you in CHRIST JESUS.

The key word in this verse is, "in all circumstances". Thanking GOD for the things He has done for us, like the abundance, protection, security, healing, graces, blessings and even answered prayers, are not enough. We have to thank GOD for the trials and tribulations, for all our problems and even for the unanswered prayers.

In our weakness and in times of distress, that's when He doubles His care. We are to depend on Him and He is the only solution to our problems.

Let me repeat, He is greater than any of our problems. So, no exception. Give your thanks in all circumstances

One time I was leading an opening prayer with a small group, and in my prayer I thanked GOD for my problems and discomfort. Then during our group discussion, one of the members asked me why I have to thank GOD for my problems? I told her that every time I have problems I learned to lean on GOD. Isn't it that we always ask for GOD'S help in our distress? The more I have problems, the more I feel He is there.

So in all matters, in every issue and in everything, we have to be thankful even for the unanswered prayers. Again, no exception. Ask GOD for the gift of wisdom and understanding, to know why your prayers are not granted.

Are you familiar with this phrase, "In His Time"? It is true that GOD works in mysterious ways, in His Time.

> LORD GOD, thank You for everything, the good things and the problems as well. We depend on Your will, LORD. I became stronger with my problems including the hurt and persecution that I encounter, and it is because of Your graces. My strength is You LORD. I pray this in JESUS' name Amen!
> 09/02/01

Bible Tidbits

SALT OF THE EARTH

2 Kings 2 : 20 - 21

20 "Bring me a new bowl", Elisha said, "and put the salt into it", When they had brought it to him, 21 he went out to spring, and threw salt into it saying, "Thus says the LORD," "I have purified this water. Never again shall death or miscarriage spring from it.

Is the nomenclature NACL familiar to you? I'm sure if you took chemistry in your school year, you'll remember that it is sodium chloride, in short, "salt".

Yes, salt is an important ingredient, condiment or seasoning in most of the food we eat and of course in cooking. Salt signifies many things. It's used in cleansing and purification as it says in the verse above.

In Colossians 4:6, it says, "Let your speech always be gracious, seasoned with salt, so that you know how you should respond to each one". So, in other words, salt is actually an ingredient for a lot of virtues, from being compassionate, being generous, and also being courteous.

The Bible called Christians the "salt of the earth". Our Christian testimonies are proofs of our being salt of the earth. Salt should be sprinkled when it is needed and this is according to GOD'S direction.

In Mark 9:50, it says, "Salt is good, but if salt becomes insipid with what will you restore its flavor? Keep salt in yourselves and you will have peace with one another." Salt is indeed an outcome of the virtues attain. Peace is the reward, (the flavor brought by being a true Christian)

Do you consider yourself, "salt of the earth"?

LORD GOD, I thank You for allowing me to be the salt of the earth. I ask Your grace and spiritual direction as to where I'll sprinkle the salt. Let me not become insipid and lose my flavor. LORD, continue to give me spiritual enrichment, all this I pray in JESUS' name Amen!
09/02/01

Esther B. Jimenez

PACKAGE DEAL

Isaiah 55 : 1

All you who are thirsty, come to the water! You who have no money, come, receive grain and eat; Come without paying and without cost, drink wine and milk.

When GOD sent His Son JESUS to redeem us, He didn't ask for payment, nor expect any favors back. He knows the extent of our sins and He knows the extent of our LORD JESUS CHRIST'S sufferings.

GOD knows that we are hungry for truth and how thirsty our souls are. That's why He also gives us the Sacraments of Reconciliation and the Holy Eucharist, thus, we receive His Body and Blood. It is indeed a package deal.

I am so thankful and appreciative and grateful for being a Catholic, because of the Sacraments and the daily mass, the adoration and other Catholic devotional rites. These help me in my spiritual growth. This is the best deal of a lifetime, "a package deal".

LORD GOD, thank You for all the Sacraments, for the liturgy, the rites, the package deal and everything. I pray all this in JESUS' name Amen!
09/02/01

THE STUMP

Isaiah 11 : 1

But a shoot shall sprout from the stump of Jesse, and from his roots a bud shall blossom.

Jesse is David's father, the shoot and the stump of the Davidic dynasty will remain, and from it will rise new shoot… "The Messianic King". The root of Jesse has blossomed through the Holy Spirit and Blessed is the fruit of Mary's womb.

I encouraged you to read all the verses in Matthew 1, (the Genealogy of JESUS). And you'll find out about the outcome of the "Stump". Did you ever trace back where you really come from? I am referring to a family tree. Did someone in your family track down your origins? It is interesting to find out how far we are able to trace our roots. I'm sure it will take thousands of generation to really know where we came from. The bottom line is, we know that JESUS is the Son of GOD and we are His children. We are part of Jesse's stump. We belong to JESUS' Dynasty, to His kingdom.

So if we are part of that tree, what are we going to do, to be productive and more deserving? Are you going to be a beautiful bud that shall blossom in GOD's kingdom?

LORD GOD, I ask that You give me the grace to be worthy of being part of Jesse's stump. Everyone of us is created in Your Image, all generations. In every generation, You are there to take care of the shoots. I pray for the welfare of the next generation. All this I pray in JESUS' name Amen!
09/02/01

Esther B. Jimenez

MODEL OF HUMILITY

Philippians 2 : 3

Do nothing out of selfishness or out of vainglory; rather, humbly regard others as more important than yourselves.

Even with my eyes closed and even maybe in my sleep, I can claim that JESUS CHRIST is the model of humility. He loves us more than Himself. He prefers to sacrifice than to use his power as Son of GOD. He washed the feet of His apostles. He serves the poor and welcomes the sinners. And He let John baptize Him.

When JESUS gives His teaching, He uses parables and He doesn't brag about His super power; and He talks to his disciples as His peers. When He heals he always request the ones He healed to keep it to themselves. Isn't this a genuine humility? This is how to imitate JESUS, His very own humility. Thomas Kempis the author of, "Imitation of CHRIST", said that JESUS wants us to remember this: "Let the eternal truth please you above all things, and let your own supreme nothingness displease you always". "Despise the world and desire Heaven". This is a wonderful message for all of us. This a holy reminder for us to be less vain or not to be vain at all.

So do we have the chance to change, to be humble like JESUS? Are we going to compare ourselves to think we are better than others? Do you want the gift of humility? Then, you have to ask GOD'S grace.

LORD GOD, I always pray for the gift of humility and I thank You for granting it to me. Again, thank You for helping me in my transformation. I also pray for the gift of prudence, to strengthen my humility. I ask this in JESUS' name Amen!
09/02/01

Bible Tidbits

THE POWER OF INTERCESSION

1 Timothy 2 : 1 – 2

1 First of all, then, I ask that supplication, prayers, petitions, and thanksgivings be offered for everyone, 2 for kings and for all in authority, that we may lead a quiet and tranquil life in all devotion and dignity.

Christians and non-Christians need prayers. Everybody in this world needs prayers. No one is exempted. Individual praying is good, but community prayer is stronger.

Remember the adage, "No man is an island"? We have to be concerned with one another.

There are different kinds of prayers. When you pray for other people, it is intercessory prayer. Again the LORD said, "if there are two or three gathered in JESUS' name, He will be in their midst". Praying for others is a very noble intention, and it shows thoughtfulness, selflessness and generosity.

Another Holy Person, with a lot of virtues and is very powerful in interceding is... our Blessed Mother, the Virgin Mary, our Mother of Intercession. She always intercedes for all of us and with us, too. So, do you have other people to pray for?

Do you limit your prayer to the family circle, or your circle of friends? How about praying for other people whom you do not know? How about praying for the people who hurt you or what we call enemies or foes?

Don't you know that someone from somewhere is praying for you, too?

LORD GOD, thank You for the gift of intercession; for the gift of prayers, for the gift of the community prayers and also for the chance that You have given me, to pray for the people who have no one to pray for them, for those who are asking for prayers. I pray for all of our intentions. All this I pray in JESUS' name Amen!
09/02/01

Esther B. Jimenez

UNDERSTANDING THE SCRIPTURES

2 Peter 3 : 15 -16

15 And consider the patience of our LORD as salvation, as our beloved brother Paul, according to the wisdom given to him, also wrote to you, speaking of these things as he does in all his letters. In them there are some things hard to understand that the ignorant and unstable distort to their own destruction, just as they do the other Scriptures.

I would like to start my reflection by writing one of my poems, entitled, "The Amazing Book".

The greatest story is in the Bible,
The Bible is the best seller in the whole world,
It tells the story of mankind and creation,
And the origin of our parents and its generation.
The Bible is a book of reference, a book of virtue, a book of knowledge,
It's a guide for everything and anything you can imagine,
The proverbs, the psalms, the canticles of the prophets,
Are just overwhelming and worth reading.
So it is not too late yet fellow readers;
Start opening your Bible, read it diligently,
Ponder from your heart, have a reflective mind,
And don't let your Bible stay on the shelf, stagnant.

Understanding the Scriptures is knowing GOD, His Son, and the Holy Spirit. So, if you want to know the Holy Trinity too, ask GOD to give you the wisdom, understanding and knowledge and He will grant them to you. LORD GOD, I offer everything to You, I pray this in JESUS' name, Amen!
09/03/01
    THE BIBLE IS YOUR LIFE, YOUR LIFE IS BIBLICAL

EXTRA TIDBIT

I mentioned in my Bible Tidbit # 68 on page 70 about "The Holy Replacements".

One of the Holy Replacements is about the changing of negative thoughts to positive thoughts…the negative attitude to positive attitude.

The sign of negative is like this (-), and just add another line vertically, then you'll have a positive sign like this (+). Now take a look at the second sign, it's a cross. The symbol of the cross will carry your negativity to triumph, the triumph with JESUS.

Let me just show you a typical example of how you can change your negative attitude to a positive attitude.

I found a flyer in a park one time and read the following poem about the rain.

It seemed it was written by someone who doesn't like rain that much. The poem read like this:

Rain, you've spoiled our picnic,
Rain, you have ruined our days,
Rain, you were not invited,
Is that why you've acted that way?

So, you've noticed the negative thoughts that this person expressed about the Rain. Now, here is my positive version of the, "Rain"

Rain, you've blessed our day,
Rain, you've given us food in a subtle way,
Rain, you were most invited,
Rain, I understand, so, don't mind what they say.

So, be positive, think positive, act positive, the result will be positive and productive.

Esther B. Jimenez

GOD'S PROMISE

For I am convinced that neither death, nor life, nor angels, nor principalities, nor present things, nor future things, nor powers, nor height, nor depth, nor any other creature will be able to separate us from the love of GOD in CHRIST JESUS, Our LORD.

Romans 8 : 38 – 39

HUMAN RESPONSE

To give oneself wholly to GOD means to:

1) Prefer His will always
2) Never take back what we have given to Him
3) Never do what displeases Him, nor omit what is pleasing to Him
4) Let Him be the absolute Master of our hearts
5) Live in complete dependence on His grace and always be docile to His divine will.

From: "The Imitation of CHRIST"
By: Thomas Kempis

APPRECIATION

My sincere gratitude, is extended to the following individuals for their efforts in making this book possible. Again, they are the completion of this book.

Elaine Ambrose
Cris de Asis
Betty Balauag
Carmina & Ely Bomediano
Celia & Terry Banez
Margie P. & George Boerema
Virgie & Eric Cabrales
Arlene Calido
Lettie Camacho
Alma Changrachang
Cora Celicious
Nancy Cirujales
Tessie Comprado
Elmie Criste
Elizabeth P. Criste
Angie & Pietro Fricano
Edith Funtera
Lucy Galleza
Terry & Roberto Gomez
Citas Gutierrez
Jean & Jhun de Guzman
Arleen & Rey Jimenez
Evelyn & Jay Jimenez
Ernie B. Jimenez
Honorata & Pedro Jimenez
Lourna & Robert Jimenez
Lydia & Rafael Jimenez
Jay & Evelyn Jimenez
Ching B. Lazo
Erlinda & Carlos Maniclang
Rosie & Ben Manogura
Carmen & Ernesto Manuel
Rick A. Mayvald
Cora & Jim Mindo

Mellie & Conrad Ortanez
Belen Oliva
Lourdes Pestano
Adelaida delos Reyes
Mely Santa Brigida
Jean & Ferdie Samaniego
Helen & Alex Santos
Doty & Hannah Soriano
Jean Mary Schummer
Zeny Valero
Remy Villalon
Cathy E. Yap
Flores Zerrudo